JOHN WITTICH

Citizen and Woolman of London

Discovering
London's Inns
and Taverns

D0556099

SHIRE PUBLICATIONS LTD

Contents

ACKNOWLEDGEMENTS

Cover design by Ron Shaddock. Photographs are acknowledged as follows: plates 1-7, Cadbury Lamb; plates 8-9, John Wittich.

Printed in Great Britain by C. I. Thomas & Sons (Haverfordwest) Ltd, Press Buildings, Merlin's Bridge, Haverfordwest.

Introduction

Towards the end of the twelfth century, William Fitzstephen, secretary to the saintly Thomas Becket, Archbishop of Canterbury, writes of London in his biography of his master. Beginning the Prologue with an elaborate dedication to Becket, Fitzstephen then comments on London and its inhabitants: 'The only plagues of London are the immoderate drinking of fools and the frequency of fires.'

The public house, a place set aside for the sole purpose of supplying drink to the passer-by, has in many ways taken the place of two distinct types of establishment — the inn and the tavern. There was always a difference between the two in law. At an inn one could obtain lodgings and meals as well as drinking the local brew of ale, whereas a tavern was a house where it was strictly forbidden to serve anything except drinks. The records show a number of innholders and tavern-keepers being fined for failing to observe the law in this matter.

The first inns, in a form we would recognise today, were a development of the Saxon ale-house; they evolved, through the medieval church-hostels, into the inns or hotels of the present day. The word *inn* is of Saxon origin; at first it meant a chamber or bedroom, but later it came to mean a suite of rooms in which one lived. An excellent example of this use is the Inns of Court, where chambers (suites) are set aside as living quarters for lawyers.

A German ambassador, who stayed in an English inn in 1129, recorded his appreciation in what must be the first visitors' book. He wrote: 'the inns of England are the best in Europe, and the Fountain, wherein I am now lodged as handsomely as I were in the king's palace, the best in Canterbury.'

The medieval inn served travellers only and provided merely the bare necessities. A guest would find an earthen floor, sometimes paved with stone slabs, and occasionally covered with rushes, although this was a luxury only provided in places where rushes were easily available; such inns that London possessed at that time would certainly not have had them. The guests slept in dormitories, shared by both sexes. The traveller would have a pallet on his share of the floor and would probably supply his own food or have some brought in from a nearby public cookhouse. The charge for the service was low. Records of journeys made by fellows of Oxford and Cambridge colleges still survive in some of the college archives. The Warden and two fellows of Merton College, Oxford, were charged one halfpenny for their beds, a farthing for candles and a farthing for soup. There were complaints about overcharging even in those days, and laws were passed to protect the traveller from being cheated.

Not only the brewers but also the Church brewed and sold ale.

The ingredients were provided by the parishioners, and the Church Ale was sold in aid of the church funds. In the records of St Peter's church, West Cheap, burnt down and not rebuilt after the Great Fire of 1666, an entry for 1447 shows that eighteen shillings and four pence was raised in this way. Hops were first cultivated in England in 1070 but not used in beer making until 1390.

An official eye was always kept on the price and quality of the beer made and sold in the City of London. In the fifteenth century Richard Whittington, four times Mayor of London, prosecuted the Brewers' Company for allowing the selling of dear ale — and won the case with costs.

In 1589 there were a thousand taverns in the City of London, and Lord Chancellor Bacon suggested that a few might be closed. Successive Lord Mayors had tried to limit the drinking but had had no effect.

The seventeenth-century diarist Samuel Pepys recorded his impressions of the inns of London and elsewhere, and Charles Dickens in the nineteenth century described the gin palaces of the day. He stated that there was one tavern to every sixty houses on average and that the gin palaces had thousands of customers daily.

The characters who have patronised the drinking houses of London can still be found there today. Their dress may belong to the twentieth century but the hospitality and the welcoming atmosphere remain unchanged.

1. Nelson and his ports of call

Standing high on his column Horatio, Lord Nelson, looks down on the inns and taverns at his feet with perhaps a little regret that his present situation no longer allows him to sample the wares of the places he knew so well in days of old.

Because of its name, and being close to the old Admiralty building, the **Ship** (1) in Whitehall makes an appropriate start to the taverns of this area. It is built on the site of the former Rummer Tavern, which in the early eighteenth century was owned by Sam Prior, the uncle of Matthew Prior, the poet. Matthew was appointed Ambassador to The Hague, in which post he contracted a number of treaties, and later acted as a spy for the Tory government. No doubt he used his uncle's tavern to further his ends in this task. Jack Sheppard, the eighteenth-century housebreaker who four times escaped from prison, committed his first crime here — he stole two silver spoons. In later years the place became popular with the leading dramatists of the time.

Turning left on leaving the Ship, the walker soon reaches the corner of Great Scotland Yard, once a palace where the Scottish kings stayed when visiting London. At the end of the street is Northumberland Avenue and across the way is the **Sherlock Holmes** (2). Of all the great characters of fiction Holmes and Doctor Watson must be amongst the most popular; interest in them is as keen today as it has ever been. It is said that Holmes was created by Conan Doyle while waiting for his patients to attend his surgery. Walks around London in search of places associated with Holmes are very popular. Here the walls of the bars are decorated with Holmes memorabilia, and objects connected with his deeds are admirably displayed in the cases. Upstairs, on the way to the restaurant, can be seen a faithful reconstruction of the front room at number 221B Baker Street, complete with the bust supplied by Madame Tussauds when it was learnt that a sniper had been hired to shoot Holmes from the upstairs window of a nearby house. Holmes sits there in front of the fire reading his copy of *The Times*. A correspondent in the American press commented a few years ago that 'until the world's press print an official obituary to Sherlock Holmes he lives on,' a sentiment with which all members of the Sherlock Holmes Society will surely agree.

A short distance along the alleyway at the side of the Sherlock Holmes, after crossing Craven Street, is the **Ship and Shovel** (3), a reminder of the coal-heavers and their nightly gatherings on the banks of the river Thames. Today it nestles beneath the brick arches that support Charing Cross railway station. The shops 'underneath the arches' are interesting to tourists and Londoners and may well form part of this walk under the shadow of Nelson. Charles Dickens once worked in a blacking factory on this site, although nothing remains of it today.

For the walker who takes the route under the arches the way leads to Villiers Street. When this is reached he should turn left towards the Strand. Crossing over the road, towards the church of St Martin in the Fields, the way leads to Adelaide Street and then William IV Street. Turn left and on the corner is the **Marquess of Granby** (4), shown on earlier maps as the Hole-in-the-Wall. Here Claude Duval, the famous highwayman, was taken captive while drunk; this was just as well, for he was armed with three pistols at the time. Under its old name the house had been kept by Mother Maberley, a mistress of the licentious George, Duke of Buckingham.

In times past the **Salisbury** (5) in St Martin's Lane, once called the Coach and Horses and later Ben Caunt's Head, after the landlord better known as the Nottinghamshire Giant, was well known for the prize fights organised within its bars. Early in the nineteenth century Jim Belcher's comeback from early retirement was arranged here against the Game Chicken; history does not record the result. With its horsehair settees and Victorian atmosphere, the Salisbury today is frequented by actors from the local theatres.

A short step from the Salisbury to New Row brings the traveller to the **White Swan** (6), a famed tavern since 1789. It has a reputation for helping ladies in distress. Charles Dickens used the tavern in several of his books. The *Epicure's Almanack* for 1815 recorded that the White Swan was a long-established house, well-known for the excellence of its fish, flesh and fowl, which were served in the best style of cookery by bill of fare daily to numerous respectable guests.

Tucked away off the beaten track is the **Lamb and Flag** (7), whose address is actually 33 Rose Street, but one is well advised to park the car and walk! For four hundred years it has been the haunt of theatre-goers and theatricals. Its sign, identical to that of the Middle Temple Inn of Court, may have been of religious origin, although exactly why here is a mystery. Like its near neigh-, bour the Salisbury, the Lamb and Flag has been closely associated in the past with prizefighters. Indeed at one time its nickname was the 'Bucket of Blood'. This is another tavern that Dickens used and knew well from his associations with the area. One of the earliest street signs was seen here with 'This is Rose Street 1623' carved upon it, and not far from the house Dryden, the playwright, was attacked by three ruffians as a result of some words he had written about Charles II's mistress.

At the junction of Garrick Street and Long Acre is sited the **Frigate** (8). A ship's figurehead ten feet high welcomes you aboard, and with the rigging swaying in the wind it is hard to believe that the site is comparatively new and that Nelson himself did not know the place.

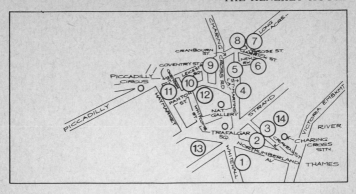

NELSON AND HIS PORTS OF CALL

1. The Ship
2. The Sherlock Holmes
3. The Ship and Shovel
4. The Marquess of Granby
5. The Salisbury
6. The White Swan
7. The Lamb and Flag
8. The Frigate

9. The Henekey House
10. Stone's
11. The Tom Cribb
12. The Hand and Racquet
13. The Two Chairmen
14. Station buffet, Charing Cross

Passing on, dropping in for a quick one at the **Henekey House** (9) in Leicester Square, the pedestrian soon finds himself in the part of the square carefully allotted to him by the City Council. Much of the square is cut off from traffic, although cars are allowed down two sides. So the wanderer comes to Panton Street and Stone's.

Though not strictly a public house or drinking place **Stone's** (10) in Panton Street is world-famous as a chop house and restaurant. Established in 1770, it should not be missed by the lover of all that is 'old and good'. Rebuilt after extensive damage in the Second World War, it combines tradition with the latest comforts and conveniences.

A few yards from Stone's, on the next corner towards the Haymarket, is the **Tom Cribb** (11). In Conan Doyle's *Rodney Stone* the Tom Cribb in Panton Street is known as Tom Cribb's Saloon because Tom Cribb was the landlord. He was a noted fisticuffs fighter in the eighteenth century and his picture is painted on the signboard on the front of the house.

Retracing your route to Whitcombe Street from the Tom Cribb, it is only a short distance to the **Hand and Racquet** (12), so called because the royal tennis court lay nearby.

By turning to the left the walker passes the Theatre Royal and

Her Majesty's Theatre before reaching New Zealand House on the corner. After crossing the roadway by way of the road island and ignoring all temptations to take the short cut back to Trafalgar Square, Cockspur Street is reached. Here, tucked away from the main stream of traffic, is Warwick House Lane. The house has long since disappeared, but the **Two Chairmen** (13) recalls a more leisurely way of travelling — by sedan chair. Inside this small public house there is always a hearty welcome to the stranger. The inn sign depicts two chairmen in seventeenth-century dress, and the panel of the door of the chair bears the royal monogram of two interlocking Cs.

It is not far back to the start of the walk or to buses, Underground trains, or British Rail trains at Charing Cross station. If using the last of these and you have time to spare for your train, there is always the **station buffet** (14) to help you while away the time.

2. Let's all go down the Strand

From the twelfth century the Strand has been the main road linking Westminster and the City of London and was once lined with the stately homes of bishops and nobles. Anyone walking down the street today will be attracted to look into the many shops there. But there are also a number of interesting places of refreshment either in or near to the street.

Beginning at Charing Cross station, pause for a moment to admire the replica of the Eleanor Cross in the forecourt of the station, then turn right outside and walk towards the City of London.

Shortly after leaving the station, turn right down Villiers Street until you come to John Street; this will lead to the **Gilbert and Sullivan** (1). It is furnished with programmes, bill posters, miniature stage sets and many other items related to the operettas of Gilbert and Sullivan. The bar on the ground floor will satisfy your thirst while more substantial food is served in the restaurant over the bar.

This area was once the riverbank and all the streets lead down to the river, which has retreated some hundred yards with the building in the nineteenth century of the Embankment. In the eighteenth century the Adam brothers reclaimed the bankside and built a series of streets and houses, calling it the Adelphi, the Greek word for brothers. One of the lanes which leads back to the Strand is George Court, where the **George Tavern** (2) now stands, reminding the explorer that this land was once owned by George Villiers, Duke of Buckingham. It is said that the Emperor Napoleon lodged in this court between 1791 and 1792.

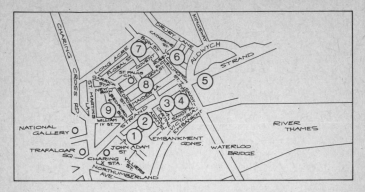

LET'S ALL GO DOWN THE STRAND

1. The Gilbert and Sullivan
2. The George Tavern
3. The Coal Hole
4. The Savoy Hotel
5. Short's
6. The Nell Gwynne
7. The Nag's Head
8. Rule's
9. The Lemon Tree

Having regained the Strand after leaving the George, turn right once more, and walk along to the **Coal Hole** (3) at the head of Carting Lane. In the early nineteenth century this tavern was a popular rendezvous for the coal-heavers who worked the Thames and who, after a long and tiring day, relaxed here in the evenings. The Wolf Room is a reminder of the club founded here by the actor Edmund Kean for repressed husbands who were not allowed to sing in their baths.

For the man-about-town who really wants to impress his girl-friend there is always the **Savoy Hotel** (4), either for a quick drink or a quiet meal. The Savoy is built on the site of the former royal palace of the Savoy, deriving its name from Peter of Savoy, whose statue stands on the outside of the hotel and who came to England in 1241. All that is left of the palace and later hospital is the Queen's Chapel Royal, built in the early sixteenth century.

Claiming to be one of the oldest wine-bars in London, **Short's** (5), just past Lancaster Place, which leads to Waterloo Bridge, was rebuilt early in the present century, although records go back to at least 1726. At that time it is recorded that a 'small house known as the Strand Hotel was acquired by a Mr Short'. His charge, in those times, was 'a shilling for an ordinary'. This was the cover charge for a meal and drink that was simply 'ordinary'.

Although some authorities disagree, Nell Gwynne, the orange-selling mistress of Charles II, may have been born in a house in a lane or alley off Drury Lane. It is appropriate therefore that the

THE NELL GWYNNE

Nell Gwynne (6) should be found here. Nell herself is buried in the church of St Martin in the Fields, and her funeral service was conducted by Thomas Tenison, the rector of the parish, who later became the Archbishop of Canterbury. She was often seen on the stage of the Drury Lane Theatre, which is situated in Catherine Street, as is the tavern that bears her name.

On the corner of James Street and Floral Street, behind the Royal Opera House, Covent Garden, is the **Nag's Head** (7). It was originally built as a hotel, drawing its clientele mainly from the opera house. Its inn sign depicts a circus horse. The interior decoration has the opera as its theme, with old playbills and designs for stage sets adorning the walls of the bars and the restaurant on the first floor. It was also patronised by the users of the Covent Garden market until the market was moved to Vauxhall. It is, however, still popular with the singers and dancers from the theatre.

Walk through Covent Garden, passing the portico of the church of St Paul, designed by Inigo Jones in the seventeenth century. Notice the plaque on the wall recording that the first Punch and Judy performance was given here, witnessed by Samuel Pepys, in the seventeenth century. Follow Southampton Street to Maiden Lane, which runs parallel to the Strand. Here is **Rule's** (8), founded in the late eighteenth century and an accepted place of call for people interested in the theatre. Its gallery of portraits is without rival in the world of the theatre and includes all the great actors from Irving and Terry to the present day.

Continue along Maiden Lane and cross into Chandos Place to the junction with Bedfordbury. You are walking in the footsteps of the famous and the infamous, for Charles Dickens frequented the area in his youth and the notorious highwayman Claude Duval was finally caught in the vicinity. Perhaps they visited the **Lemon Tree** (9). Lemons were first introduced into England in the fifteenth century, but this public drinking house does not date back that far in history. Its nearness to the old Covent Garden fruit and flower market may well account for its name. In the *Daily Advertiser* of 6th April 1742 the Lemon Tree in Bedfordbury is mentioned as the place to enquire about the letting of a chapel in Great Queen Street — a strange role for a drinking house!

From here it is a short walk back to Charing Cross station and other public transport services.

3. Drink in the street of ink

The history of Fleet Street goes back to Roman times. It was once called Fleet Bridge Street for it led to the bridge over the river Fleet, and on up Ludgate Hill to St Paul's Cathedral and beyond.

But before we come to Fleet Street itself we must not ignore the eastern end of the Strand.

An original oil painting of George III incorporated into the facade of the **George** (1) explains how the inn acquired its name. It was rebuilt in the late nineteenth century and the architect created so perfect a Gothic building that many tourists must have mistaken it for a genuine medieval pub! It is well worth studying the outside before sampling the goods for sale inside. Notice particularly the care that has been taken in creating the right atmosphere by including delightful carvings in the timbers of the building. A statue of Dr Samuel Johnson shares an island in the roadway with the parish church of St Clement Danes. He stands, dictionary in his hand, looking down Fleet Street towards his favourite inns and taverns.

Leaving the George, turn left outside and walk along to Essex Street to the **Edgar Wallace** (2). This may still be known to many people as the Essex Head, taking the name from Robert Devereux, Earl of Essex, a former owner of the land and house here. In 1975, the year of the centenary of the birth of Edgar Wallace, the public house was renovated and renamed the Edgar Wallace. The illegitimate son of an actress in Greenwich, Wallace became a famous war journalist, author of some of the finest crime stories ever written and a playwright both for the stage and for films. He died in 1932 and his body was brought back from Hollywood, where he was writing screenplays, and buried in the tiny church-yard at Little Marlow in Buckinghamshire. Photographs, facsimiles and other mementoes are shown on the walls of the bar and the upstairs restaurant. Literary dinners, at which his daughter, Penelope, gives a short talk about the life and times of her illustrious father, are regularly held here.

Leading out of Essex Street, to the side of the Edgar Wallace, is Devereux Court, on the inner corner of which stands the **Devereux Arms** (3). It was originally the Grecian Coffee House, patronised by Steele, who wrote his learned articles here. Today the clientele consists largely of men of the law, their students, and others who have bothered to discover this charming oasis behind the hustle and bustle of the Strand and Fleet Street. It first appears under its former title in a list of coffee houses published early in the eighteenth century and acquired its present name about a hundred years later. High above the main entrance to the house is a bust of a later Earl of Essex with the inscription 'This is Devereux Court, 1676'.

Not open to the general public but nevertheless a building to take note of in the walk is the **Wig and Pen Club** (4). Built in the early seventeenth century, it is a good example of a house that existed in London before the Great Fire of 1666. Today it is one of the best eating and drinking clubs in London, whose members, in the main, are all connected with the law or writing. Chivalry and the rules of the club still demand that a lady shall not be left alone in any of the bars, and if necessary a male member of the staff will keep a lady company until her own escort returns. From the windows of the club an excellent view of the Lord Mayor's Show can be gained. The club stands just outside the City of London, whose boundary is marked by a monument in the middle of the roadway here, on the former site of Temple Bar.

Walking down Fleet Street away from Temple Bar, you will find **Ye Olde Cock Tavern** (5). Originally on the opposite side of the roadway, it was rebuilt on its present site in 1887, when the street was widened. All that is left of the former house is the inn sign said to have been carved by the seventeenth-century woodcarver Grinling Gibbons. Pepys, Thackeray and Dickens all knew the house and recorded their visits to it. Samuel Pepys mentions a particularly comely wench, a certain Mrs Knipp. Like those of other public houses in the City, the hours of opening do not coincide with national licensing hours. Closing time here is usually nine o'clock in the evening, and the place is closed on Saturdays and Sundays.

A City Corporation blue plaque marks the site of Dr Johnson's favourite tavern, the Mitre in Fleet Street, but just behind, in Mitre Court, there is the **Clan** (6), a building of the twentieth century but with ancient associations. Here a hearty welcome awaits the thirsty passer-by. If you are in the vicinity on the night before a rugby international, come here and sing your heart out, and quench your thirst as well. By day the Clan is the haunt of the 'men of the law and their students'.

El Vino's (7), once described as being frequented by judges, QCs and the upper crust of journalists, is not strictly speaking a tavern or an inn but a place of good refreshment. Dylan Thomas, the Welsh poet, was a constant visitor during his time in London. The house is still a social centre for Fleet Street, and its distinctive Victorian atmosphere belies the fact that it was only built in the early decades of the twentieth century. This is because most of the furniture and fittings come from the company's property built in Mayfair in 1879 and removed here early in this century.

Perhaps the most famous of all the inns and taverns of Fleet Street is **Ye Olde Cheshire Cheese** (8) with its long connections with Dr Johnson and other literary figures. It was rebuilt shortly after the Great Fire of London in 1666, but the site is much older and covers the cellars of the house of the Abbots, later Bishops, of Peterborough. One of the most famous inhabitants of the inn was a parrot whose knowledge of abusive words was second to none. Its fame was widespread and people came from far and wide to listen to it speak. When it died, in 1926, at the alleged age of forty years, obituaries appeared in leading newspapers throughout the

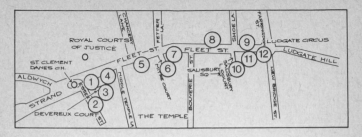

DRINK IN THE STREET OF INK

1. The George
2. The Edgar Wallace
3. The Devereux Arms
4. The Wig and Pen Club
5. Ye Olde Cock Tavern
6. The Clan
7. El Vino's
8. Ye Olde Cheshire Cheese
9. The Poppinjay
10. The Old Cogers
11. The Bell
12. The Punch

English-speaking world and also in the *North China Star*: 'Famed bird of blasphemy dies...victim of pneumonia'. Even the BBC mentioned it in its newscasts. Dr Johnson's chair is still there, but there is little else to remind the visitor of the illustrious customers of the past.

A few yards down the road from Ye Olde Cheshire Cheese is a new public house, opened in 1976, the **Poppinjay** (9). It is built on the site of 'the sign of the popyngaye' — the sign of the Abbots of Cirencester, whose house stood here in medieval times. Every May the Festival of the Poppinjay took place in the fields outside the city wall. A model bird was attached to a pole and used for target practice by archers.At the end of the day the winner was declared to be Captain Poppinjay. The stone in the entrance to the house weighs two and a half tons and is made out of red Mansfield stone from Nottinghamshire. It formerly stood over an archway leading to Poppins Lane nearby.

True lovers of the English pub may care to make a slight diversion from the trail at this point to visit the site of a former public house, the **Old Cogers,** formerly called the Barley Mow, in Salisbury Square (10). The building, designed by Sir Edwin Lutyens, architect of the Cenotaph in Whitehall, is now used for other purposes but was once a good place of refreshment. Its later title comes from the eighteenth-century debating society which used the house for its weekly meetings. They have now moved their sessions to the Welsh Harp, Temple Lane, where they still function under the name of Ye Ancient Society of Cogers. Members of the public are admitted to observe their strange customs, including the one that stipulates that the main speaker must always make some reference to the Royal Family during his opening speech in the debate, but only members of the society are allowed to participate in the debates.

Return to Fleet Street once more and remain on the right-hand side of the roadway and soon you will come to the **Bell** (11), with entrances both in Fleet Street and in the tiny lane that runs beside the nearby church of St Bride. During the rebuilding of the city after the Great Fire of London priority was given to the quick reconstruction of many of the inns and the Bell was one of these. It still quietly serves the needs of its clientele, whether passers-by or members of the choir from the nearby church.

No visit to the pubs of Fleet Street is complete without a call at the **Punch** (12), particularly if you are a great admirer of the cartoons and articles that appear in *Punch* magazine, which has entertained thousands of people for very many years.

Finally you reach Ludgate Circus, with the memorial plaque to Edgar Wallace on the corner of Farringdon Street, and all the pubs of the City of London before you.

---

4. Jack London's abyss and the Ripper's haunts

Arriving in London at the turn of the century Jack London, the American novelist, made an intimate study of the area of the City 'just beyond Aldgate'. He used the information he obtained from his survey to form the basis of his novel *The People of the Abyss*, telling of the dreadful conditions under which the poor working-class people of London lived. Murders, rape and other violent crimes were commonplace, but none has captured the imagination of the public as much as the crimes committed by Jack the Ripper. Between August and November 1888 five prostitutes were murdered in the most brutal manner, and although several names have been suggested, including that of a member of the Royal Family, nobody was ever brought to trial for the crimes. Today the area is changing, but the atmosphere of the dank, gaslit Victorian streets can still be found by those with a nose for the unusual.

Purporting to be one of the oldest surviving licensed houses in London, the **Hoop and Grapes** (1) was built in the seventeenth century, but originally served as a private house. The construction of the building is typical of the houses of the period and conveys something of the atmosphere of the city before the Great Fire destroyed five sixths of London in 1666. Notice the carving on the newel post at the entrance, the overhanging upper storeys, and, on entering the building, the narrowness of it. The bar and the

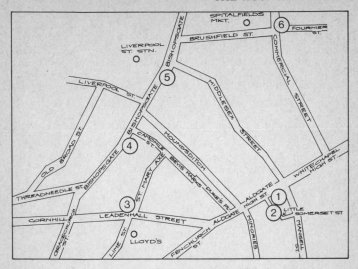

JACK LONDON'S ABYSS AND THE RIPPER'S HAUNTS

1. The Hoop and Grapes
2. The Still and Star
3. The Underwriter
4. The Magpie and Punch|Bowl
5. Dirty Dick's
6. The Jack the Ripper

kitchen are connected by an ear-shaped device in the wall, the forerunner of more sophisticated modern methods by which the barkeeper can communicate with the kitchen staff. Under the building there are sprawling cellars and passages, which are said to have linked the house with the Tower of London, or perhaps with the docks where smugglers and river pirates held sway. Over one of the window frames can be seen the parish boundary marks of the parishes of St Botolph's, Aldgate, and St Mary's, Whitechapel.

Hidden from the sight of the passer-by in Aldgate High Street, the **Still and Star** (2) is well worth searching out. It is in Little Somerset Street, a place linked with Jack the Ripper by those who think he may have been a butcher at one of the slaughterhouses in the neighbourhood. The origin of the name is obscure, although the Still may merely show that an apparatus for distillation was once kept here. It is certainly a rare name for a public house, although there is one in Sleaford, Lincolnshire, bearing the sign of the Still. The second half of the name may be explained as the sign of the Innholders' Company — the Star of Bethlehem that shone over the inn.

Both Lloyds and the Baltic Exchange are in the parish of St Andrew Undershaft, so it is not surprising to find the **Underwriter** public house (3) underneath the comparatively new development area that houses the Commercial Union Assurance Company and the P & O Line shipping company. Underwriters are in this instance men who insure a ship or its cargo for an agreed amount of money against loss and are so called because their name is written under the policy document.

Leaving the Underwriter, crossing behind the Commercial Union building and passing St Helen's church on your right, you re-enter the hustle and bustle of the city's busy streets through the archway that leads into Bishopsgate. Turn right and you will soon come to the **Magpie and Punch Bowl** (4) on the corner of Clarks Place. If you wander up the side of the building, with its Bridges and Estates Committee badge, you will discover the blue plaque recording the site of the first hall of the Worshipful Company of Parish Clerks of the City of London (time has changed the e into an a in the street name). The Clerks almost certainly frequented this house in days of old. It was towards the end of the seventeenth century that taverns began to adopt the name of Punch Bowl, when punch became a popular or, rather, a fashionable drink. Punch was far more popular a drink with the Whig party than with the Tories, whose tastes were more for sack, claret and canary. The punchbowl nearly became the party badge of the Whigs, and taverns bearing this name have almost without exception had political allegiances towards the Whigs in the past. Magpies were considered to be lucky birds and were therefore often chosen as the name of a tavern.

Leaving the walled city of London by passing through the site of the old Bishopsgate, with the bishop's mitre on the wall just beyond Camomile and Wormwood Streets, but still remaining within the jurisdiction of the Lord Mayor, the walker soon reaches **Dirty Dick's** (5), in Bishopsgate. According to the story, Nathaniel Bentley sealed up the room in which his wedding breakfast was to have taken place after his bride to be left him waiting at the church and became a ragged eccentric instead. The room was later bought by the landlord of the tavern in Bishopsgate that today bears Bentley's nickname of Dirty Dick. Legend has it that Nathaniel had inherited the family hardware business from his father, had attended the court of Louis XVI of France and become 'a most accomplished courtier' but was rejected by his bride to be. Although Bentley lived and died in Leadenhall Street, the landlord is supposed to have moved the room, lock, stock and barrel, to this place in Bishopsgate; the previous tavern on the site was called the Gates of Jerusalem or the Old Port Wine House. It is well worthwhile descending to have a drink or two in the dirtiest circumstances imaginable.

From Bishopsgate take the second street on the right-hand side, Artillery Lane, and follow it until you reach the junction with Artillery Passage. Here stop and admire the recently restored eighteenth-century houses and shops, noting particularly the one with the old wooden fire-pump engine inside. Across the roadway there is a multi-storey car park, the entrance to which is in White's Row. On the opposite side of the street to the car park there is a seventeenth-century house restored to its former glory but no longer used as a residence. White's Row leads into Commercial Street; turn left and shortly the parish church of Spitalfields, Christ Church, designed by Nicholas Hawksmoor in the eighteenth century, is seen on the corner of Fournier Street. It looks across the street to the **Jack the Ripper** (6). Formerly called the Ten Bells, the Jack the Ripper is another of London's theme pubs, where the decor is related to a particular subject. Here the walls are adorned with photographs of the places where the Ripper murdered his victims and with extracts from the *Illustrated Weekly Police* newspaper. It is generally accepted that there were five murders by the same person called Jack the Ripper; all five victims had their throats cut and were disembowelled. All were prostitutes and in their forties, except the last, Mary Kelly, who was also the only victim to have been murdered inside; the rest were left on the public highway.

The neighbourhood around the Jack the Ripper is interesting to explore but, for those wishing to return to the bright lights, the street opposite the church, Brushfield Street, will bring them shortly to Bishopsgate and Liverpool Street station.

5. Along Old Father Thames's north bank

It has often been said that London's history is the story of its river, the Thames, and there are many old and interesting inns and taverns on its banks. To get to know them all would require a lifetime, but some are particularly inviting to the drinker and to the historian.

Standing right on the edge of the Thames at Isleworth, the **London Apprentice** (1) commands a very good view of the river and has as its neighbour the parish church, whose tower dates from medieval times, though the rest of the building is modern because the previous church was burnt down by fire caused by young children playing with matches. A short distance away is the entrance gateway to Sion House, the London home of the Dukes of Northumberland, rebuilt in the eighteenth century to the designs of Robert Adam, the Scottish architect. Dominating one side of the inn is a painting of the London apprentice, who having spent the afternoon rowing on the river stopped and refreshed himself at the inn. Rebuilt in the early eighteenth century, with a stucco ceiling in the upstairs lounge well worth going to see, today it is a scheduled building of great architectural interest, and although it no longer stays open all night as it did in earlier days its popularity is as great as ever.

There are several attractive riverside inns and taverns at Chiswick's Strand on the Green. If you approach the Green from Kew Bridge, the first port of call is the **Steam Packet** (2), a reminder of the ships that plied for hire on the river in the nineteenth century. To travel by boat was then the cheapest and safest way, with far less chance of being robbed on the water than on the land.

The next tavern stands by the towpath. It is the **City Barge** (3), and its sign clearly shows the reason for its name. The river here was used to moor the barges of the Lord Mayors of London, in times when they, too, found the river to be the safest way of travelling. The river sometimes overflows its banks along this stretch so that the water laps against the walls of the inn. Consequently precautions have been taken to prevent flooding inside the building: there is a step before entering the bar, and at high tide beams are placed in a slot on the outside of the door frame. The licensees of the City Barge have charters which show that the original house on this site was built in Elizabethan times. However, the site may be older still, for references to the City Barge at Chiswick occur in fifteenth-century documents. To have visited the inn five hundred years ago on a cold night would have been a pleasure; warm beer was served, heated by a red-hot poker from the open fire placed into the tankard, and with a generous helping of ginger added. The bar is dominated by the seventeenth-century Parliamentary Clock with its open face. If there had been a hinged glass door on the face a tax would have had to be paid to the Government, so the face was left uncovered.

Leave the City Barge, turn left outside the riverside bar and walk along the towpath once again. The railway bridge carrying Underground trains to Richmond is soon seen, and shortly beyond it is the **Bull's Head** (4). Apparently a nineteenth-century building, it actually consists of two cottages of the early eighteenth century knocked into one. Rumour has it that the cottages were used as a secret hideout by Oliver Cromwell during the seventeenth century but no work of this date survives today.

Downstream from Chiswick is the former village of Hammersmith, originating from a small hithe, or inlet in the riverbank, used for the loading and unloading of goods from boats. At the end of Hammersmith Mall, a continuation of the Chiswick Mall, is a group of seventeenth- and eighteenth-century houses served by

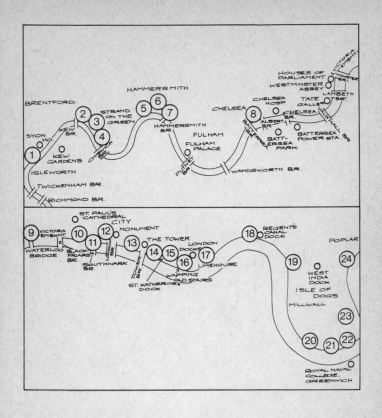

ALONG OLD FATHER THAMES'S NORTH BANK

1. The London Apprentice
2. The Steam Packet
3. The City Barge
4. The Bull's Head
5. The Dove
6. The Rutland
7. The Blue Anchor
8. The King's Head and Eight Bells
9. The Caledonia
10. The Samuel Pepys
11. The Riverside Restaurant
12. The Old Wine Shades

13. The Tiger Tavern
14. The Tower Hotel
15. The Dickens Inn
16. The Town of Ramsgate
17. The Prospect of Whitby
18. The Grapes
19. The City Arms
20. The Robert Burns
21. The Ferry House
22. The Waterman's Arms
23. The Cubitt Arms
24. The Gun

the **Dove** (5) — strictly, it is in the Upper Mall. It was purchased by its present owners, Fuller, Smith and Turner, in 1796, and there was a riverside inn here in the seventeenth century. There is a grapevine near the verandah, which is a favourite place to watch the annual Oxford versus Cambridge boat race, during which beer drinking is interrupted for a short time while the customers forecast the result of the race. William Morris lived in the house almost next door to the pub and so the Pre-Raphaelite artists were frequent visitors to the place, which appears in some of their paintings. In more recent years A. P. Herbert used the Dove, disguising it as the Pilgrim in his novel *The Water Gypsies*. 'Rule Britannia' is said to have been written in an upper room of the house. A plaque in the public bar shows the height of the high tide of 1928, and it is to be hoped that this mark will never again be reached. Brian Lovrey's inn-sign, over the main entrance of the building, shows the dove and the rainbow, although, through a mis-spelling in the nineteenth century, the pub has been known as the Doves. Nell Gwynne and Charles II are said to have frequented the inn in the seventeenth century.

Turn right outside the Dove and a short path leads to the riverside, Furnivall Gardens, Hammersmith Pier and the first close sight of Hammersmith Bridge. Along this stretch of the riverbank are several places of refreshment — rowing is a thirsty sport — including the **Rutland** (6) and the **Blue Anchor** (7). Both attract visitors to their doors during the summer and conveniently provide seats for patrons who like to watch the river and its activities while drinking.

Chelsea has many attractions and one of its numerous places of refreshment is the **King's Head and Eight Bells** (8), on Cheyne Walk. The name arose from the fact that long ago it was the custom to ring the church bells when royalty was travelling on the river in the vicinity. Here, too, the overflow of people from the bars spreads out on to the pavement in the summer season.

The **Caledonia** (9) provides a chance to drink on board a paddle steamer that used to cruise on the Scottish lochs but is now moored at the Victoria Embankment in the heart of London. There is a selection of bars, both inside and out, from which the drinker can enjoy splendid views of the river, with pleasure steamers passing by on their way downstream to the Tower and Greenwich and barges moving upstream carrying cargoes of coal or oil.

Soon the City of London is reached, with its numerous places of refreshment. Amid the redevelopment of the Castle Baynard area, in a nineteenth-century warehouse building, is the **Samuel Pepys** (10). The lower bar is decorated as a seventeenth-century ship's chandlers. At the restaurant, for which advance booking is advisable, the menu includes 'Samuel Pepys's favourite dinner' —

roast beef and Yorkshire pudding — served by young ladies who certainly would have met with Pepys's approval. In the supper bar and on the verandah are displayed quotations from the famous diary that Pepys kept, with particular reference to the Great Plague of 1665 and the Great Fire of 1666. Here, too, you may sit and watch the river flow by. Look out when the tide is right for the 'flat-iron' boats that can still be seen carrying their loads up and down the river. Formerly they used to have to lower their funnels every time they approached a bridge, but the diesel-engined craft of today have no need to do this.

It is but a short walk to the end of Southwark Bridge and the **Riverside Restaurant and Bars** (11). It is a modern building, but from the restaurant there are good views over south London and lunchtime crowds eat and drink on the riverside balcony. One of London's most famous taverns, the Anchor, can be seen from here nestling under the shadow of Cannon Street station's railway bridge over the Thames.

Return to Upper Thames Street and continue to walk towards the Tower of London. Amid modern office developments, in the quiet of Martin Lane, is El Vino's the **Old Wine Shades** (12). It was built over three hundred years ago and miraculously survived the Great Fire of London of 1666 and the Blitz of 1940-1, although it is but a stone's throw from where the Fire started in a baker's shop in Pudding Lane. Here you may partake of your favourite sherry, port or other kind of wine. Charles Dickens was a frequent visitor here and enjoyed its old-world atmosphere as much as the citizens of today. Evidence of its pre-Fire origin is provided by the finely decorated lead cistern, which bears the date 1663. Early maps and writings refer to the house as the 'Sprague Shades', presumably after a former owner or licensee. A tunnel, now blocked, led down to the river and must surely be a relic of the smuggling that went on here.

At the end of the longest street in the City of London, Thames Street (Upper and Lower), is the Tower of London, and the **Tiger Tavern** (13) is opposite its main entrance. Founded in the sixteenth century, though rebuilt in the twentieth century, this tavern has a long and most interesting history. In the upper bar can be seen, by pressing a light switch on the wall, a mummified cat said to have been stroked by the young Princess Elizabeth when she was imprisoned in the Tower. There are still remains of a tunnel that she used to reach the tavern under the moat and roadway, though both ends have now been securely blocked. Every ten years an interesting ceremony takes place here: the Lord Mayor of London, the Sheriffs, Aldermen and members of the Common Council come here, bringing with them their beer-tester to test the quality of the beer being sold. It is not by any modern scientific means that the test is made: some of the beer is poured on to a stool, provided by the inspectors, and the tester then sits on it. If the man's breeches are stuck to the seat all is well — and it always is! When the ceremony is completed a garland is placed round the neck of the landlord and a bouquet of laurel leaves is hung outside the door.

Beyond the Tower of London a new development has arisen over the past few years centred round the **Tower Hotel** (14), which has several restaurants and bars open to the general public. A new vista of the Thames has been opened up, from Tower Bridge downstream towards Greenwich. Many boats are moored in the marina, including several historical vessels such as the old *Nore* lightship and some sailing barges with their red sails.

Amongst the many eating places and shops in this area is the **Dickens Inn** (15), in a converted building previously part of a brewery in St Katharine's Dock. Opened in 1976 by the great grandson of Charles Dickens, the inn is a place of unusual interest. Its ground-floor bar serves only real ales, with not a single bottle in sight, while the upper floors provide food. On the top floor, in the famous Dickens Room, are held cabarets which have a special Dickensian theme.

Now that most of the trade of the London docks has moved downstream to Tilbury many acres of land here have become derelict over the past few years. Next to St Katharine's Dock is the London Dock, now disused, but between the river and the dock Wapping High Street still runs. By going along St Katharine's Way and crossing the entrance to the London Dock the High Street is soon reached and just past the entrance to Wapping Basin is the **Town of Ramsgate** (16). Previously shown on maps as the Red Cow in deference to the colour of a former barmaid's hair, it was renamed the Town of Ramsgate after being adopted by the Ramsgate fishermen who used to sell their fish from Old Wapping Steps at the side of the public house. It was on these steps that 'Bloody' Judge Jeffreys was caught, disguised as a sailor, when trying to escape to Hamburg. He was recognised and taken to the Tower of London, where he died of wasting disease. He was buried secretly in the church of St Mary Aldermanbury. When the church building was dismantled to be rebuilt in America the judge's grave was discovered, but the site has not been marked. Sailors found guilty of crime on the high seas were sentenced to death by being washed over by three tides at this point of the river. The water bloated the bodies, and the expression 'What a wapper' is said to have originally referred to somebody executed in the river here at Wapping.

Seen from the river or from the land the **Prospect of Whitby** (17) seems a small public house. Originally built in 1520, it is one of the oldest riverside public houses and was once known as the Devil's Tavern after its associations with the river thieves and smugglers.

Samuel Pepys visited the place a number of times and in the upper room, known as Pepys Room, the Ancient Society of Pepys still holds its meetings, while on the wall hangs a seventeenth-century chart of the port of Harwich inscribed 'To ye Honbl. Samuell Pepys, Esq., Secretary of the Admiralty of England, etc'. Later in the same century 'Bloody' Judge Jeffreys came here to watch the river executions, and in the nineteenth century Charles Dickens used the Prospect as the Six Jolly Fellowship Porters in *Our Mutual Friend*. By Dickens's time the name had been changed from the Devil's Tavern to the Prospect of Whitby. The change came about because a ship called the *Prospect*, which was registered at Whitby in North Yorkshire, was moored off the tavern. The ship became a landmark and the tavern was referred to as the one by the *Prospect* of Whitby, and so this eventually became its name. In the early eighteenth century a sailor brought into the bar a flower that was then unknown to the local inhabitants. He sold the plant to a local market gardener, who used it to produce three hundred like it. The plant was the fuchsia and is still very popular with gardeners all over Britain. Here, too, came the artists Whistler, Turner and Dox to paint the beautiful sunsets over the river, and doubtless they sampled the brew of the tavern before they left.

From the Prospect of Whitby on Wapping Wall go back to The Highway and turn towards Stepney. When Narrow Street appears on the right-hand side walk down it and there you will find the **Grapes** public house (18). Like the Prospect of Whitby, it is situated beside the river, has an attractive verandah and claims to be the model for Charles Dickens's Six Jolly Fellowship Porters in *Our Mutual Friend*. The building dates from 1650, but the place is first mentioned in local records in the sixteenth century. A short distance from the house the Regent's Canal joins the river Thames.

The next bend in the river brings the explorer to the Isle of Dogs, which contains no fewer than twenty-two places of refreshment within its bounds. The Isle acquired its strange name because the royal dogs from the palace of Greenwich, across the river from the Island Gardens, were kept here, away from their royal owners, who doubtless wanted to enjoy quiet nights undisturbed by the noise of the dogs howling. Enter the Isle by West Ferry Road and you will find the **City Arms** (19) on the right-hand side of the road. Decorated in modern style, its great attraction, apart from its beer, is the metal sculpture of the Great Fire of London.

Continuing down the road, and regrettably having to pass several public houses on the way, you reach the **Robert Burns** (20), whose name is a reminder that many Scotsmen helped build Brunel's steamship, the *Great Eastern*, on the banks of the river here. The site is marked but can only be seen from the river itself.

Where the West and East Ferry Roads meet turn right and then almost immediately left into Ferry Street and find the **Ferry House** (21). It is a reminder of the ferry that used to carry passengers and horses across the Thames from Greenwich to the Isle of Dogs before the Greenwich Foot Tunnel was built in 1902. The nearby steps to the river are still called Horse Ferry Steps. From here it is a short walk to the Island Gardens, from where there is a fine view across the river to Greenwich and the Royal Naval College, Greenwich Park and the Queen's House.

Shortly afterwards you come to Glengarnock Avenue and the **Waterman's Arms** (22) with its splendid Edwardian decor and fine collection of items connected with old-time music halls. Collectors' pieces from the world-famous Collins Music Hall on Islington Green in north London were brought here, as were many other priceless objects from the good old days of live theatre and variety shows in the nineteenth and early twentieth centuries.

It is hardly surprising to find the **Cubitt Arms** (23) on the Isle of Dogs, for many of the buildings were the work of Thomas Cubitt, the noted nineteenth-century architect.

The **Gun** (24), in Cold Harbour, Poplar, brings to an end our search along the northern bank of the river Thames for inns and taverns of historical interest. It makes an ideal place from which to watch the comings and goings of the craft on the river. It is situated at the entrance to the West India Dock, but the earliest reference to the house is in the fifteenth century, long before the dock was built. Lady Hamilton owned a cottage in this then rural area, and Lord Nelson is said to have stayed at the Gun while courting her.

---

6. Meat market and thirsty porters

One of the largest meat markets in the world, Smithfield is built on land that was once the open 'smooth field' outside the City of London's great wall. Fairs regularly took place there, including the great St Bartholomew's Fair held each year until the late nineteenth century, when it was stopped because it had become too unruly.

First established in 1695, **Henekey's Wine House** (1) in Holborn was the first of a chain of houses which originally sold only wine. The present building has extensive cellars, which were put to good use in the times of the anti-Catholic Gordon Riots of the eighteenth century. Dickens has David Copperfield in temporary residence in the gatehouse to Gray's Inn, next door to the tavern. A triangular fireplace in the centre of the room appears to have no chimney: the smoke escapes from the fireplace by way of a

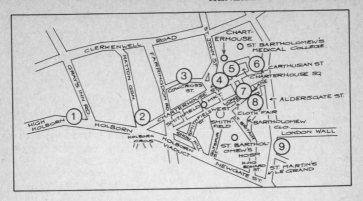

MEAT MARKET AND THIRSTY PORTERS

1. Henekey's Wine House
2. The Mitre
3. The Castle
4. The Smithfield Porter
5. The Fox and Anchor
6. The Sutton Arms
7. The Red Cow
8. The Hand and Shears
9. The Raglan

chimney under the floor. If you want to show your prowess at drinking then there is a yard-glass at your disposal. All you have to do is to drink the contents down in one go without pausing for breath or spilling any on the floor.

Turn left outside Henekey's and walk along the road towards the City of London, whose boundary is marked here, at Holborn Bars, by dragons holding the coat of arms of the City between their paws; this was the place where visitors to and from the City were checked and tolls were paid. It marks the limit of the jurisdiction of the Lord Mayor of London. Shortly after entering the City you will see the red brick building of the Prudential Assurance Company. At one corner of this is Leather Lane, whose street market attracts local residents and thousands of office workers every day from Mondays to Fridays.

Sitting on his horse, with his hat raised in the air, is Prince Albert, Queen Victoria's Prince Consort, said to be the politest statue in the whole of London. Here also is Hatton Garden, famous the world over for its diamond merchants; and just to the side an old lamp-post points the way to the **Mitre** (2), Mitre Place. It takes its name from the headgear of a bishop and dates from 1547. It stands on land once owned by the Bishops of Ely, whose town house stood nearby. It is said that Queen Elizabeth I threatened to unfrock Bishop Richard Cox if he did not give the house and land to her favourite, Sir Christopher Hatton. In one

25

corner of the bar there is a tree trunk said to be the remains of a cherry-tree around which Elizabeth I danced. At one time this tavern observed the licensing hours of Cambridgeshire and this was very convenient when they did not coincide with the London hours. Even now the Mitre's hours are slightly different and it is best, in the evening, to check before you visit to make sure how long you have left for drinking!

If you leave the Mitre and turn left you shortly enter Ely Place, which is a private road and not patrolled by the City police. Up to the Second World War (1939-45) a beadle walked the street after dark and called out the time and the condition of the weather for the benefit of anybody who happened to be awake. Passing through the wrought iron gates, turn left again and walk down Charterhouse Street until you reach the junction of Farringdon Road and Farringdon Street, between which the dragons of the City stand guard once more.

Turn left up Farringdon Road, then right along Cowcross Street, and passing Farringdon Underground station on the left, cross over to the **Castle** (3). George IV is said to have been attending a cockfight nearby one day early in the nineteenth century, when he ran out of money. Having a sure winner in the next round, he went to the Castle and persuaded the landlord to loan him five pounds, using his father's watch as a security. The king won the next bet and returned the money to the landlord, who, it is claimed, had not recognised the king. The landlord was offered a knighthood, which he refused, but he did accept the right to act as a pawnbroker. The three brass balls still hang in the bar, but whether you can hock anything today remains to be seen.

Following Cowcross Street round, you will find yourself at the back of the Smithfield Market; here there is a group of public houses which have a special dispensation allowing them to serve market workers between 6.30 a.m. and 9 a.m. This privilege does not extend to ordinary members of the public.

The sign of the **Smithfield Porter** (4) clearly shows the dress of a porter in days long since past and is a valuable source of information to the student of historical dress. Dressed in his long smock-like overcoat and complete with his flat-topped hat, the porter is ready for the day's work ahead.

In the little side road that leads to the beautifully peaceful Charterhouse Square is the **Fox and Anchor** (5). Before entering read the notice on the outside regarding the 'market holden at Smithfield'.

When the local Charterhouse monastery was dissolved in the reign of Henry VIII the property was bought by Thomas Sutton, a lawyer who had a passion for travel. He later became Elizabeth I's Master of the Ordinance and used the monastery as almshouses for retired men, a use which continues to this day. The **Sutton**

Arms (6) in Carthusian Street is a reminder of his great benevolence.

A short walk away is Long Lane; John Stow wrote that it was 'truly long'. Here is the **Red Cow** (7), a pleasant small nineteenth-century building, frequented by the thirsty porters of the market.

From beside the Red Cow a short lane leads to Cloth Fair and the **Hand and Shears** (8), where a tavern has stood for four hundred years or more. Here the Court of Piepowder (dusty feet) was held and the stallholders from the nearby market and fairs could settle their differences of opinion. Weights and measures used at the market were brought here to be tested. Offenders and fraudulent traders were fined or otherwise dealt with in accordance with the law of the times. Here, too, came the Lord Mayor of London to declare open the famous Smithfield fair by cutting the first piece of cloth to be sold. From this custom comes the present-day practice of cutting a piece of tape or cord when declaring open a new bridge, road or building. The traders, however, usually managed to start the proceedings themselves in an entirely different way the night before in the many taverns in the area.

After walking the entire length of Little Britain, you will reach Aldersgate, at the far end of which is the **Raglan** (9). It occupies one of the oldest hostelry sites in the City of London; Shakespeare knew the previous house well during his stay in London in the sixteenth century. Originally known as the Bush, it was changed to the Mourning Bush after the execution of Charles I by its Royalist landlord, who also painted the inn-sign black. After the Crimean War of the nineteenth century it was once again renamed — this time after one of the heroes of the conflict, Lord Raglan. Its cellars survive from the original house and incorporate parts of the old Roman wall and the city gate of Aldersgate.

7. Up west around the 'Dilly

A piccadill was a collar ruff made in the seventeenth century, and a certain tailor who sold piccadills at his shop in the Haymarket built himself a house nearby and called it Piccadilly Hall. The place was described as being 'a fair house for entertainment and gaming, with handsome gravel walks, and an upper and lower bowling green', and it gave its name to the street in which it stood.

In the street immediately behind the Criterion Theatre, Jermyn Street, is to be found the **Cockney Pride Tavern** (1), though one is unlikely to hear the bells of Bow church from inside the tavern and so claim to be of Cockney stock. The visitor will be invited to view the collection of 'what the butler saw' machines and will be able to order 'puddings and mash', for which the place is rightly popular.

Turn right outside the Cockney Pride and, crossing over Lower Regent Street, continue to walk down Jermyn Street until St James's church, Piccadilly, appears on the right-hand side of the roadway. Opposite the church is Duke of York Street. At number two is the **Red Lion** (2), a fine example of the nineteenth-century 'gin palace', with its mirrored walls and cast-iron spiral staircase leading from the bar to the toilet. A past winner of the *Evening Standard's* Pub of the Year Award, it is rewarding today for the company to be found there as well as for the beer it serves.

Now return to Jermyn Street and continue away from the church towards St James's Street, but before reaching the end of the street turn left into Duke Street, St James's. Here is to be found the **Chequers** (3) public house, but before entering look up for a moment at the inn-sign showing the chequered board used for playing either draughts or chess. Both of these games were once very popular with the people who frequented alehouses in days of old, and the sign was also used in medieval times by moneychangers. Behind the tavern in Mason's Yard is the seventeenth-century building used by the royal masons for stabling their horses. The pub is the gathering point for members of the Water Rats, the showbusiness people's charity.

Returning to Piccadilly itself for a visit to the **Yorker** (4), opposite the Royal Academy building, is well worthwhile whether one is an addict of cricket or not. The house is a museum to the noble game of cricket and certainly should not be missed by the visitor to the area.

By this time the drinker may welcome a short walk in search of the next pub. Return to Jermyn Street again and walk along to Bury Street. At the other end of this street is King Street, and diagonally opposite is the old Crown Alley. Walking down this alley is like stepping back in time, for it is a charming eighteenth-century back-street: on the right-hand side are small shops with shutters and iron bars to keep them secure when the staff have gone home. At the end of the alley stands the **Red Lion** (5), once described as the former alehouse standing in Crown Alley. But the gardens mentioned in the original lease of the building have disappeared, nor is there any sign of the secret passages that are said to link the tavern with the nearby St James's Palace. Perhaps these were the reason why it is called Crown Alley. It is not impossible that a king might have used the place as a rendezvous with a mistress, and Charles II's mistress, Nell Gwynne, did have a house nearby in Pall Mall.

The alley leads to Pall Mall, but by turning right the walker soon reaches St James's Street. At the other end is Bennet Street, in which is the **Blue Posts** (6). The place is mentioned by the Restoration dramatist George Etheridge in 1677 as an alehouse from where blue-coloured sedan chairs could be hired. Posts, also

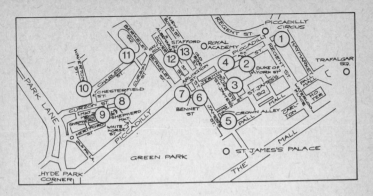

UP WEST AROUND THE 'DILLY'

1. The Cockney Pride Tavern
2. The Red Lion, Duke of York Street
3. The Chequers
4. The Yorker
5. The Red Lion, Crown Alley
6. The Blue Posts
7. The Ritz Hotel
8. The Bunch of Grapes
9. The Shepherd
10. The Red Lion, Waverton Street
11. I Am the Only Running Footman
12. The Duke of Albemarle
13. The Goat Tavern

painted blue, were to be found in the old courtyard here at the side of the horse troughs, and it is from these that the public house, rebuilt after being bombed in the Second World War, was named. Inside the house the publican keeps, as a showpiece, one of the blue sedan chairs; it should be noted that it is not for hire or sale!

Arlington Street, to the side of the public house, leads to Piccadilly and the **Ritz Hotel** (7), which has licensed bars, where those who would like a change from drinking in public bars may enjoy the quiet seclusion of the hotel. Only hotel residents will be served with drink after the licensing hours. When an attempt was made a few years ago to pull down the hotel and redevelop the site protests were made, and the hotel is now a Schedule A protected building and cannot be altered externally, although improvements may be made to the rooms.

It is a short walk down Piccadilly to Half Moon Street, at the end of which is Curzon Street and the **Bunch of Grapes** (8), nestling in the corner of Shepherd Market. It was built as the Market Coffee House in 1736 when Edward Shepherd was developing the area, the site of the once notorious May Fair, with shops and houses. Although doubtless grapes were sold in the market and fair, the inn-sign was originally used to denote a wine house as opposed to an ale or beer house.

29

Diagonally opposite the Bunch of Grapes is the **Shepherd** public house (9), named after the founder of Shepherd Market. Inside the house is a sedan chair, now used as a telephone kiosk, that was once owned, and doubtless sat in, by George II's son the Duke of Cumberland. There is also a collection of Chinese porcelain in the bar, while the attractive exterior of the building is in the style of the Georgian period, with light green and gold offsetting the bottle glazing of the small bow windows. It is an eighteenth-century pub with a difference and certainly worth a visit.

The **Red Lion** (10) in Waverton Street is as old as the Shepherd, both having been built in the mid eighteenth century. It has been described as a country house in the heart of London and one hundred years ago it served as a farmhouse. A pair of Dick Turpin's pistols is on show in the bar.

From the Red Lion walk along Charles Street and at the far end of the street, at the junction with Hay's Mews, is the **I Am the Only Running Footman** (11). The job of this servant was to run ahead of his master's coach to warn the tollkeepers of the impending approach of the coach, pay the necessary toll and then to hurry on to the next tollgate. In the seventeenth and eighteenth centuries the strength and endurance of these servants of the aristocracy was prodigious: it is recorded that they could run between sixteen and twenty miles in little over two hours. The running footman carried in his hand his wand of office, which contained his refreshment consisting of red wine and the white of eggs mixed together to sustain him in his often long and tedious journeys. There is no other public house named after these servants of the residents of Mayfair.

Cross the southern side of Berkeley Square, walk up Hay Hill into Dover Street and turn right. On the next corner, on the left-hand side of the street, is the **Duke of Albemarle** (12). Inside there is an original street-name sign reading 'This is Stafford Street 1686'; although there has been a house on this site since that time the present building dates from the twentieth century. The Duke is also commemorated in the nearby street that bears his name. The Duke was granted a plot of land by the grateful monarch, Charles II, at the Restoration of the Monarchy in 1660, but the area was laid out by Sir Thomas Bond.

Further along Stafford Street is the **Goat Tavern** (13), with a life-size goat as its inn-sign. In 1736 a trust was set up here for the benefit of the needy of the two local parishes. Rent is still paid to this fund.

To return to Piccadilly from the Goat, turn left outside the house, walk along to Albemarle Street, then turn right and very shortly Piccadilly is reached.

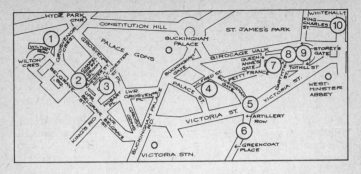

BELGRAVIA AND SOUTH-WEST ONE

1. The Grenadier
2. The Horse and Groom
3. The Talbot
4. The Colonies
5. The Albert

6. The Greencoat Boy
7. The Architectural Press
8. The Two Chairmen
9. The Westminster Arms
10. The Red Lion

8. Belgravia and South-west One

The **Grenadier** (1) in Wilton Row can be approached either from
Wilton Place, by turning left into Wilton Crescent, after which it is
the first on the left, or from Grosvenor Crescent, which runs by
the side of St George's Hospital, Hyde Park Corner; turn into
Wilton Crescent and find Wilton Row on the right. Here the Duke
of Wellington stabled his horses and a mounting block is pointed
out as having been used by him. Appropriately the theme of the
tavern is the Army; moreover Old Barrack Yard is close by and the
house is haunted by an officer of the Grenadiers who was caught
cheating at cards. Altogether the Grenadier is one of the most
charming refreshment houses in Belgravia.

Return to Grosvenor Crescent and walk towards Belgrave
Square; this land was reclaimed from swamp by Viscount
Belgrave, a member of the Grosvenor family. (Belgrave is a small
hamlet on the family's estates near Chester.) Much of the soil used
for this work came from the newly dug docks of east London.
Cross the square by the side leading directly out of the Crescent
and shortly Chapel Street appears on the left-hand side. Enter this
street and you will come to Groom Place. The **Horse and Groom**
(2) is a delightful nineteenth-century house and it is hard to think
of the area as once being associated with lepers and a hospital, the
Lock Hospital, for ladies of easy virtue who had contracted 'the
dreaded disease'. Stables were often found at the rear of the

elegant houses of the fashionable squares of the eighteenth century, and with them went horses and grooms — hence the pub's name.

Cross Chester Street by way of Wilton Mews and Little Chester Street will be found running parallel. Here is the **Talbot** (3), a reminder of a hunting dog now extinct but an ancestor of the present-day bloodhound.

Between the Talbot and the next port of call, the **Colonies** (4), there are a number of taverns that might well entice the walker inside. But the Colonies in Wilfred Street should not be missed. Built in the colonial style, it is decorated with skins and trophies from the golden days of the British Empire.

At the end of Wilfred Street is Buckingham Gate and where the latter joins Victoria Street stands the **Albert** (5). Although its future was once in great doubt, it has defied progress and survived the redevelopment of the area. In the days when the first meal of the day was not a rushed affair between getting up and rushing off to catch a train to the City, they served large English breakfasts here. Prince Albert, consort of Queen Victoria, looks down from the signboard on all who enter. Downstairs the gas lighting has recently been restored and the first-floor room is dominated by portraits of two other great Victorians, Disraeli and Gladstone.

In the days of charity schools the children who attended them were distinguished by the colour of their coats. Blue, grey and green coats were to be found in this area, though only the Grey Coat Hospital (school) survives today, but the **Greencoat Boy** is remembered in the public house that bears his name (6).

A short walk away in Queen Anne's Gate can be found the **Architectural Press** (7), which has in its basement relics from a large number of public houses, mostly destroyed in the Second World War. The relics were gathered together by Sir John Betjeman, the Poet Laureate. This is a public house without a licence to sell alcoholic drinks.

At the end of the same street, where it joins Dartmouth Street, is the **Two Chairmen** (8). It seems quite natural that the Two Chairmen should be found in an area of eighteenth-century elegance. With a little imagination one can still picture a lord and lady arriving at one of the beautiful houses of Queen Anne's Gate or enjoying themselves at the nearby cockpit while their sedan-chair attendants waited for them in the nearby tavern.

Follow Old Queen Street to the far end and Storey's Gate is reached. Here is the **Westminster Arms** (9), displaying the coat of arms of the family of the Dukes of Westminster.

Finally, a short walk along Great George Street to Parliament Street brings the walker to the **Red Lion** (10), with its Edwardian atmosphere and its connections with Scotland Yard and the Metropolitan Police, now removed to finer quarters in Victoria

1. The Wig and Pen Club in Fleet Street is not a public house but a private club whose members are mainly lawyers or writers.

2. The Poppinjay public house stands on the site of the house in Fleet Street of the medieval Abbots of Cirencester, whose sign the bird was.

3. *The Magpie and Punchbowl in Bishopsgate. The punchbowl was a symbol of the Whig party and is suggestive of the tavern's past political allegiance.*

4. The Jack the Ripper in Commercial Street is one of London's theme pubs. The decor commemorates the unknown murderer of five prostitutes in 1888.

5. The Hand and Shears near Smithfield was where the Lord Mayor
came to open the Smithfield fair. The Court of Piepowder
was held here to solve disputes between the itinerant traders.

6. The Magpie and Stump in the Old Bailey. The previous inn on the site, called the King of Denmark, was a popular vantage point for watching the public hangings outside Newgate Prison.

7. *Ye Olde Watling, established in 1666, stands in Watling Street surrounded by the tall office blocks of the City.*

8. The unique sign of the pub called I Am the Only Running Footman commemorates the servant whose task was to run ahead of his master's carriage to pay the tolls.

9. The London Apprentice stands by the Thames at Isleworth. It was built in the early eighteenth century and the stucco ceiling of the upstairs lounge is particularly fine.

Street, and with Charles Dickens, who records in his unfinished autobiography going into a public house in Parliament Street and ordering a glass of ale. David Copperfield also visited the tavern and asked for a glass of the 'Genuine Stunning'.

9. Drinking by the Thames's south side

Commanding a fine view of the finishing line of the annual Oxford and Cambridge Boat Race the **Ship** (1) at Mortlake dates back to the time of Elizabeth I, although the present building was erected during the reign of George I in the eighteenth century. Shown on the maps as the Hart's Horn, it became the Blue Anchor in the seventeenth century, before adopting its present name in the nineteenth century. There is evidence of a ford across the river nearby, and doubtless this was a good place to refresh oneself before or after crossing the river. It is an attractive public house catering for family trade.

From the Ship the roadway leads to the riverside towpath and to the **White Hart** (2), with its pleasant Victorian exterior. It is situated on a great curve of the river, and from the house a splendid view of the Boat Race can be obtained.

Pass under the Barnes railway bridge, still keeping along the riverside, to reach the **Bull's Head** public house (3). Standing on the site of a farmhouse owned by a family from the north of England, the Lowthers, the family of the Earls of Lonsdale, the present building was erected in the nineteenth century. At that time the inn was a coaching station, and the stables have recently been converted into a restaurant; many of the old fittings have been retained and incorporated in the decor. The arms of the Worshipful Company of Butchers of the City of London, the landowners, are to be found on the wall of the house. Popular pub games, such as darts, shove-halfpenny and dominoes, contribute to the atmosphere of the place.

At the other end of the Boat Race course is Putney, where the **Star and Garter** (4) is right on the river's edge. It contains memories of races won and lost, but its greatest prize on show is a pewter tankard that was washed up on the riverbank by the Surrey Dock in 1951. It bears the inscription 'Star and Garter, Putney, 1750'.

Rowing enthusiasts should not miss the **Coach and Eight** in Upper Richmond Road (5), with its colour scheme of light and dark blue, oars on the ceiling, the college shields of Oxford and Cambridge along the picture rail, and pictures of races of the past. Other sporting exhibits include items connected with the famous Doggett's Coat and Badge race, the oldest annual sporting event to be held on the river Thames. In the 1877 Boat Race the two crews were judged to have finished in a dead heat, and the prow of the Cambridge boat on that occasion is on show. This public house is a living museum to a great sport — all in a house that once showed a coach with eight horses on its sign.

Between the Coach and Eight and the **Old Swan** at Battersea (6) the riverside scenery is very varied, with houses in one place, a distillery in another, and further on a brewery; then the remains of the charming riverside village of Battersea come into sight. Standing in the shadow of the parish church of St Mary — the present building was erected in the eighteenth century — the Old Swan was first mentioned in 1215, when the watermen who rowed King John's rebellious knights and barons to Runnymede used this riverside inn as a place of refreshment. Scenes in Thomas Dibdin's operetta *The Waterman* take place in a room of the tavern overlooking the river. In 1969 a fine modern building was constructed, incorporating many huge timbers from the hulls of old Thames sailing barges (a craft of this type is usually moored nearby).

Shortly after the railway bridge in Nine Elms Lane, Thessaly Road will be found on the right-hand side. A few hundred yards along it is the **Butchers Arms** (7), displaying the coat of arms of the Worshipful Company of Butchers of the City of London. The interior decoration consists of butchers' knives and cleavers, thus creating an atmosphere appropriate to the name.

Just beyond the complex new road junction at Vauxhall Cross, near Vauxhall railway station, the road becomes the Albert Embankment, another reminder of the Prince Consort of Queen Victoria, and here stands the **Old Father Thames** (8). The Old Red Cow that once stood on this site has gone and in its place this far more sophisticated house has been built. It has a commanding view of the river from the Tate Gallery to the Houses of Parliament and its neighbour is the London Fire Brigade headquarters, and so the pub receives the attention that it deserves.

While the Albert Embankment continues along its riverside course, the roadway diverts and becomes Lambeth Palace Road, passing the gatehouse of Lambeth Palace, the London home of the, Archbishops of Canterbury, with its magnificent Tudor towers.

At the junction with Westminster Bridge Road, beside the modern extension of County Hall, is the **Geoffrey Chaucer** (9), formerly called the Pill Box. It was renamed after the fourteenth-century poet whose *Canterbury Tales* bring to life the pilgrims who set out from Southwark to the shrine of Becket.

Aptly renamed during 1977, the year of the Silver Jubilee of Queen Elizabeth II, the **Jubilee** (10) in York Road was previously called the Ordnance Arms, after a small arms depot that used to be close by.

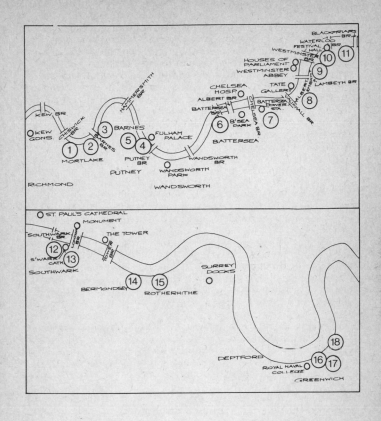

DRINKING BY THE THAMES'S SOUTH SIDE

1. The Ship
2. The White Hart
3. The Bull's Head
4. The Star and Garter
5. The Coach and Eight
6. The Old Swan
7. The Butchers Arms
8. The Old Father Thames
9. The Geoffrey Chaucer
10. The Jubilee
11. The Doggett's Coat and Badge
12. The Anchor
13. The George
14. The Angel
15. The Mayflower
16. The Trafalgar Tavern
17. The Yacht
18. The Cutty Sark

Nestling by the side of Blackfriars Bridge is the **Doggett's Coat and Badge** (11), part of a recent riverside development. It is an appropriate name for a splendid site. Thomas Doggett was an Irish comedian who came to live in London in the latter part of the seventeenth century. He instituted the race now called Doggett's Coat and Badge to commemorate the accession to the throne of George I. It is rowed over a course of 4½ miles (7.25 kilometres) from Chelsea to London Bridge towards the end of July each year. The winner receives a scarlet coat and silver badge. The decoration of the house includes a life-size figure of the coat and badge, while on the walls are displayed paintings of the barges of the City livery companies.

The way to our next public house takes us through a most interesting part of south London — Bankside. After leaving the Doggett's Coat and Badge walk down Blackfriars Bridge Road, turn left into Southwark Street, and shortly after passing under the railway bridge turn left again into Hopton Street. Follow this road round to the riverside, passing the Bankside Power Station and a house with a plaque declaring that Sir Christopher Wren lived here. Pass under Southwark Bridge, once a toll bridge but now freed from tolls by the City of London which owns it, and so reach the **Anchor** (12). It was once surrounded by warehouses, but there has been much redevelopment in the area. The present building, rebuilt in the seventeenth century, replaces the one patronised by William Shakespeare, whose Globe Theatre was just round the corner in Park Street. Here, gently supping a glass of Empress of Russia stout, which is a mixture of ale, beer and twopenny (a pale, small beer first brewed in eighteenth-century London, of lesser gravity than other beers, and costing two pence a pint), one can easily imagine the inn when it was used by river pirates and smugglers, or perhaps by a prisoner escaping from the nearby Clink prison to disappear into one of the many hiding holes that are said to exist in the Anchor. Tales are told also of the notorious press gangs who raided the house looking for healthy young men to force to join the Royal Navy. Upstairs in the restaurant, looking through the eighteenth-century window, you can watch the lights of the City of London being turned on in the office buildings. The licensee has provided a jetty over the riverbank where it is possible to eat and drink while watching the river pass by.

The walker has a choice of two routes to reach the next port of call, the **George** (13). The direct route is by way of Park Street, then along Stoney Street and down the Borough High Street to the tavern. However, for the more adventurous, the way to take is under the railway arches opposite the Anchor; then follow Clink Street between empty and forlorn warehouses until Cathedral Street is reached; then pass to the side of the Borough Market and, once again, under the railway arches to reach Bedale Street, and so to Borough High Street. The George is the last of the galleried coaching inns of London which can show its visitors some of the glory that appertained to coaching inns in the heyday of horse-drawn transport. During the seventeenth and eighteenth centuries coaches departed regularly from here to the villages around London. William Shakespeare and his fellow actors drank here as well as at the Anchor. John Stow, writing in the late sixteenth century, mentions documents, now in the Public Record Office, that contain the plans of the building of 1552; this house was destroyed by fire in 1677. The building that survives today replaced it, though part of it was destroyed at the beginning of the twentieth century when the railway companies needed extra room for their goods traffic. During the summer months companies of actors and actresses perform plays by Shakespeare on the loading bay, much as their forebears performed in the courtyards for the pleasure of the guests. Charles Dickens's Little Dorrit lived in nearby Marshalsea Prison and was married in the local church of St George; she wrote a letter to Clennan from the George. Dickens must have known the tavern well from visiting his father in the prison.

In Rotherhithe Street hard by the riverside is the **Angel** (14); a fine view of the river and the City of London towards Tower Bridge can be had from the back rooms and balcony. Its original title was the Salutation, but this was considered too religious and so after the Reformation its name was changed to the Angel, although doubtless the Angel was the angel of the Salutation of the Blessed Virgin Mary, and the inn has retained this title ever since the sixteenth century. It is built on piles over the river and there are trapdoors in the floor that must have proved very useful to the river pirates and smugglers, who could thus enter and leave the house without being seen by the forces of the law. Samuel Pepys, Secretary to the Navy Office in the seventeenth century, records in his diary that he visited the inn.

At the junction of Rotherhithe Street and St Mary Church Street stands the **Mayflower** (15), which has been the centre of the life of the parish since the sixteenth century, when its name was the Shippe. In 1611 Captain Christopher Jones moored his ship, the *Mayflower*, close by the tavern. Doubtless the talk of the tavern in those days was the news of the New World across the Atlantic and the founding of the colonies in America. Some ten years later, when the *Mayflower* returned to home waters, the captain was taken ill and died at Rotherhithe. He is buried in the parish church near two of his partners, John Moore and Richard Gardener. The restored building today recreates the atmosphere of the seventeenth century and is said to incorporate parts of the *Mayflower* within its structure. It is one of the very few inns licensed to sell postage stamps, American ones as well as British because of its close associations with the United States. The jetty commands a fine view of the river and is a very pleasant place to sit and watch the river and the boats.

The former fishing village of Greenwich has some interesting public houses nestling around the parish church, naval college and the great open space of Greenwich Park. Standing on the site of the former George public house is the **Trafalgar Tavern** (16), rebuilt in 1837 and renamed in honour of the great sea battle won by Lord Nelson in 1805. In between times the building has been used by the nearby Royal Naval College as living quarters, as a home for old seamen and from 1915 to 1965 as a men's club, known as the Royal Alfred Aged Merchant Seamen's Institute. At its restoration it reverted to the name of Trafalgar Tavern. Members of Parliament used to meet here for 'Ministerial Whitebait Dinners' during the summer Parliamentary recess, a time when whitebait was in season. Whitebait is no longer caught in the river Thames off Greenwich but, in season, it appears on the menu of the tavern. A founder member of the Institute of British Architects and Secretary of the Architects Club, Joseph Kay, designed the present building while he was Surveyor of Greenwich Hospital.

Almost next door to the Trafalgar Tavern is the **Yacht** (17), which has stood here for at least three hundred years. The Greenwich meridian line runs through the building, adding another unusual item to the interest of the place. Many tales have been told about the house since the first Queen Elizabeth sailed by to enjoy the comfort of Greenwich Palace, where she was born and for which she had a lifelong affection.

The **Cutty Sark** (18) was the Union, Ballast Quay, at the end of Pelton Road when the maps of the nineteenth century were drawn, and even then it had been there for over two hundred years. Now it has been renamed in honour of the great clipper ship, the *Cutty Sark*, which stands in the dry dock on the other side of the Royal Naval College. The house was first built in the seventeenth century, when from the upper windows fine views over the river, both towards to the spreading dockland and to the open marshes of the other bank, could be had.

10. Pretty Polly Perkins land

Whether Polly Perkins really lived in Paddington and was wooed by the milkman or not need not concern us too much as we walk through the area in search of a few pleasant houses in which to have a drink and pass the time of day with any of the locals who happen to be around.

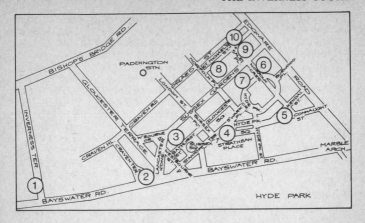

PRETTY POLLY PERKINS LAND

1. The Inverness Court
2. The Swan
3. The Archery Tavern
4. The Victoria
5. The Duke of Kendal

6. The Fountains
7. The Monkey Puzzle
8. The Polly Perkins
9. The Royal Exchange
10. The Great Western

Edward VII brought his mistress, Lily Langtry, to Inverness Terrace and the **Inverness Court** (1) and wooed her here. He had a theatre built for her within the house, where she could perform and entertain him and his friends. Today the house is a hotel functioning both as a tavern and as an inn, for there is a public bar and one can both eat and sleep here if one wishes.

Further down the Bayswater Road is the **Swan** (2), its sign proudly declaring that it was established in 1775. It stands on part of the site once occupied by Sir John Hill's physic garden, a popular place of entertainment in the eighteenth century, but no serious rival to Vauxhall or Cremorne Gardens. In later years it became the Floral Tea Gardens and was painted by Paul Sandby; a watercolour in the British Museum print room shows the unspoilt rural appearance of Paddington parish at that time. In another painting Sandby shows two low tiled buildings, in front of which are a wooden fence and a small drinking trough, and a bridge over the Westbourne river nearby. The house still retains much of its charm, and its pleasant forecourt makes a happy gathering place for locals and visitors during the summer months.

In the reign of George III the **Archery Tavern** in Bathurst Street (3) supplied refreshment not only to the people who lived nearby but also, in the early nineteenth century, to members of the

Toxophilite Society — the archers. There must have been considerable open space here then for the archers to practise in the fields around the house. The original stables and courtyard of the old inn have long since disappeared, although there are stables with horses for hire in the mews behind the public house. After relinquishing their land here, the Royal Toxophilite Society moved their butts to Regent's Park until early in this century, when they returned to south Paddington and used the former burial ground of St George's, Hanover Square, in the Bayswater Road. But that site was sold and flats and garages were built on it, so the society once more left the district.

At the end of Strathean Place stands the **Victoria** (4), with its reconstructed bar from the old Gaiety Theatre in the Strand and its distinctive Victorian decor to entice every Charles Dickens addict from miles around to pay a visit. The restaurant is Our Mutual Friend, and one likes to think of Dickens, who at one time lived in the Bayswater Road nearby, visiting the place as his local, or just for the sake of obtaining atmosphere and characters for his books. In a restoration a few years ago a painting came to light which, after having been carefully cleaned, was revealed to be of a past member of the Royal Family; it was presented to Her Majesty the Queen and now forms part of the Royal Portrait Collection.

Opened in the 1820s, the **Duke of Kendal** (5), at the junction of Kendal and Connaught Streets, is dedicated to Prince Leopold, Duke of Kendal, whose marriage to Crown Princess Charlotte brought him into the British Royal Family. He later became the first King of the Belgians, and Queen Victoria's favourite uncle. Because the house stands at the junction of two roads the bar is triangular in shape, adding to its charm.

In the 1960s much of south Paddington was redeveloped: the grand old houses of the nineteenth century were torn down by the landowners, the Church Commissioners, and new high-rise flats have taken their place. Part of the site has become the Water Gardens, complete with fountains and gardens, and a brand-new public house, the **Fountains** (6), completes the scene.

Sussex Gardens, previously called Grand Junction Road and the New Road, was part of London's first official bypass, originally formed in the eighteenth century as a route for the animals going to Smithfield. Today the **Monkey Puzzle** (7) is to be found there, complete with its monkey puzzle tree, or Chile pine, in the forecourt. It replaced the Mitre which stood where Devonport Flats now stand. The Mitre was an appropriate name as much of the land in Paddington was owned by the Bishops of London.

One must visit the little back streets between Sussex Gardens and Praed Street to find the **Polly Perkins** (8). It is in St Michael's Street on the corner with Bouverie Place. The inn-sign shows the young lady wearing her uniform as a serving maid at the local big house. Whether Polly ever existed outside the songwriter's imagination or whether she was based on a real-life figure is still a subject of debate. Certainly the song keeps alive the memory of the old village green of Paddington, much of which has long since been built over by speculative builders.

A favourite quotation from Shakespeare's play *Richard III* appears on the inn-sign of the **Royal Exchange** (9), on the corner of Sale Place and St Michael's Street. The sign shows the king, on his knees, offering the crown of England to a country yokel with the most feeble-looking horse that can be imagined, while above the picture the words 'A horse, a horse, my kingdom for a horse' explain its significance.

Being near the terminus of the Great Western Railway at Paddington station, Praed Street has a number of railway taverns; the one on the corner of Sale Place, the **Great Western** (10), shows on its sign three steam locomotives of the former GWR, in the livery of the company, reminding visitors of the glorious days of the railways, before electricity and diesel took over from coal and sweat.

11. Happy hunting ground — Soho

The word *Soho* was the password at the battle of Sedgemoor in 1685, the last major battle fought on English soil; it was the English equivalent of the French hunting cry of 'tally-ho', but it has today come to mean the area of London notorious for its strip-shows and sleazy cinemas and the saucy side of life. It is an area full of interest for the wanderer with time to look for the unusual, as well as for those wishing to find a place of refreshment with a story attached to it.

Leave Piccadilly Circus by way of Glasshouse Street, passing the Regent Palace Hotel, unless you are ready for a meal, in which case this is as good a place to eat as any in the area. Walk on to Brewer Street, to the **Crown** (1), a house much frequented by Charles Dickens and mentioned in his book *Nicholas Nickleby*, in which Newman Noggs is 'always found or heard of at the Crown'.

Walk along Brewer Street until Lexington Street appears on the left, and walk the entire length of that street to reach Broadwick Street and the **John Snow** (2). It was formerly called the Newcastle-on-Tyne, presumably from a former owner's connections with that city, but the title deeds only go back to 1927. Information posted on the walls of the bars recalls how in the nineteenth century a local doctor called John Snow traced an outbreak of cholera to the pump here and persuaded the vestry to remove the handle in order to prevent the local inhabitants from using the well while it was contaminated. Further examination revealed that the brickwork of a drain under number 40 was defective and sewage was seeping into the source of the water supply.

It was a former inn, the King of Poland, that gave its name to Poland Street, which leads from Broadwick Street to Oxford Street. At No. 23 is the **Olde King's Arms** (3), the original arms being those of James II; the stained glass windows display the Lion of Scotland and the Fleur-de-lis of France. During the eighteenth century a meeting took place here which led to the revival of the Ancient Order of Druids in Britain. Dating from pre-Roman times, the Druids combined priestly, judicial and political functions. Their origins are obscure, but the movement spread throughout Europe and across the Atlantic to America. The name 'Druid' may mean 'oak', and oak trees grew in abundance here until the seventeenth century, when many of the streets were laid out by Gregory King.

Leading to Berwick Street from Poland Street is D'Arblay Street, which takes its name from Mme D'Arblay, who as Fanny Burney spent part of her childhood near here. From here it is not far to Wardour Street and St Anne's Court, which in turn leads to Dean Street. In Dean Street is the **Nellie Dean** (4), complete with the good lady by the stream and the watermill of the famous song. However, the street name has nothing to do with Nellie Dean. The street was named after Dean Compton of the Chapel Royal, who later became Bishop of London in the seventeenth century and whose connections with the area are purely ecclesiastical.

Also in Dean Street is the **Crown and Two Chairmen** (5); it was so called because Queen Anne sat for her portrait by Sir James Thornhill in his studio opposite. Doubtless while the artist was hard at work with his painting the bearers of the queen's sedan chair were busy quenching their thirst in the public house opposite. At one time the tenant was a certain Richard Moreland, who is supposed to have been the last landlord in London to wear a pigtail and top boots. Here George Sala first met Thackeray, and he records that he sang 'The Mahogany Tree' in the small club room over the bar.

Bateman Street nearby soon leads to Frith Street and 'the only pub in Frith Street', the **Dog and Duck** (6). In the days of hunting in the area there would no doubt have been a pond or two where duck were to be found, and the dog was the means of retrieving the duck once it had been shot by the hunter.

A short walk from Bateman Street by way of Frith Street leads into Soho Square. Frith Street was the place from which John Logie Baird in 1926 transmitted the first television picture. From the square Sutton Row leads out into Charing Cross Road and so brings the walker to the very busy road junction with Tottenham Court Road and Oxford Street. At the end of Tottenham Court Road is the Dominion Theatre, now a cinema, and its neighbour,

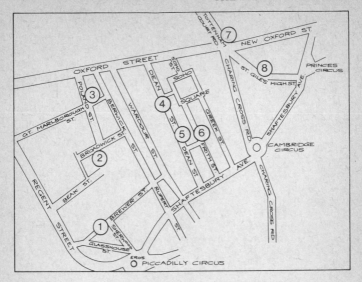

HAPPY HUNTING GROUND — SOHO

1. The Crown
2. The John Snow
3. The Olde King's Arms
4. The Nellie Dean
5. The Crown and Two Chairmen
6. The Dog and Duck
7. The Horseshoe Hotel
8. The White Lion

the **Horseshoe Hotel** (7), whose history begins in the seventeenth century, though it has been rebuilt completely since that time. There are two suggestions as to how it received its name. The first is that the brewery next door had a horseshoe nailed above the entrance doorway, and the second that once the main dining room had a horseshoe-shaped table. The brewery has long since disappeared but when it was still in existence an enormous vat, said to be capable of holding 3,555 barrels of liquid, burst its sides, and poured out its contents over the neighbourhood. Eight people died as a result, either by drowning or by suffocation.

Many thieves, murderers and martyrs had reason to be thankful for the **White Lion**, St Giles High Street (8), because it was here that they received their last drink on earth, a draught of ale known as St Giles' Bowl, to fortify them on their journey to the gallows that stood at the junction of Tottenham Court Road and Oxford Street or further to the notorious Tyburn gallows, which could be used to hang twenty-four people at once. Near this site in the seventeenth century a family contracted the plague, and neighbours, fearing that they too would catch the disease, moved to Westminster; from here, in turn, their neighbours moved into the City of London. So the Great Plague of 1665 started and was spread by the careless movement of two or three families from one place to another, and many thousands of people died during that one fatal year.

12. From Newgate to Billingsgate

During the second century AD the Romans enclosed the city of London with a wall that stretched from the Tower of London in the south-east round through Aldgate and Cripplegate to Newgate and Ludgate, a distance of over three miles. One of the most important gates in those times was Newgate, which, despite its name, was one of the earliest gates built by the Romans. Billingsgate was never a fortified entrance into the city but a dock or hithe — an inlet into the riverbank where goods could be safely unloaded from ships. Tradition has it that its original owner and builder was a local king or merchant by the name of Belling or Billing. The story says that on his death, in an unspecified year, he was cremated and his ashes were placed in an urn, which was then put on top of the gate that divided the river from the dock. Recent excavation revealed the medieval dock and, although the site has been filled in again for redevelopment, a full record has been made for posterity.

Opposite the Central Criminal Courts, commonly called the Old Bailey (they stood in the *ballium*, or open space outside the city wall), is the **Magpie and Stump** (1). The present building was erected during the twentieth century, but the site has a history almost as long as that of the Old Bailey. The Magpie and Stump was its original name, but it changed to the King of Denmark, doubtless because the husband of Queen Anne was Prince George of Denmark and many of the courtiers were Danish; at this time several streets changed their title, too. In the 1930s it reverted to its original title, the Magpie and Stump. Until public hangings were finally abolished in 1868 the house was a favourite position for wealthy City merchants and others to watch the proceedings from the upper windows. The amount charged for breakfast and a window with a view varied from £10 to £50. The popularity of such spectacles was enormous: on one occasion forty thousand people came to watch. On that day twelve people were killed in the panic caused by a pie-man stumbling among the crowd. The landlord of

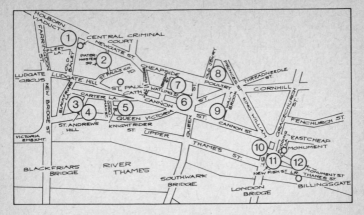

FROM NEWGATE TO BILLINGSGATE

1. The Magpie and Stump
2. The Christopher Wren
3. The Cockpit
4. The Baynards Castle
5. The Horn
6. Ye Olde Watling
7. Williamson's
8. The Three Crowns
9. Deacon's
10. The Square Rigger
11. The Canterbury Arms
12. The Cock Tavern

the Magpie fared well that day for, after the crowds had departed, he collected several cartloads of shoes, coats, petticoats and hats from the ground surrounding the execution site, while during the hangings the public house itself served as a first-aid casualty post. The crowds which frequent the public house today include lawyers, detectives, jurors and others appearing at the Old Bailey opposite.

On the north side of the Old Bailey is a City Corporation blue plaque stating that Newgate stood on the site until its demolition in the eighteenth century. This is our way into the walled City of London.

In the new office development on the south side of Newgate Street is to be found the **Christopher Wren** (2), an appropriate title for a place of refreshment so near to the architect's greatest work, St Paul's Cathedral, where he lies buried in the crypt. The pub is immediately behind another building designed by Wren, the Chapter House of the cathedral, while across the road from the cathedral is the Deanery, also by him. The son of the rector of a Wiltshire parish, East Knoyle, Wren went to Westminster School and later to Wadham College, Oxford, where he studied mathematics and astronomy. Having found favour with the king, Charles II, he was offered the post of surveyor to the port of

Tangiers, which the king had recently acquired through his marriage to Catharine of Braganza; he declined the post but instead accepted the position of Deputy Surveyor to the King's Works. After the Great Fire of London in 1666 Wren was called upon to design a new cathedral and numerous churches for the City of London. In addition he designed the Monument near London Bridge to commemorate the catastrophe, and Temple Bar was also rebuilt during the seventeenth century to his plans.

Continuing through the Paternoster development, or St Paul's Precinct as it has now been named, you reach the cathedral by way of a short flight of steps. Opposite is Deans Court, with the Deanery on the right-hand side, and at the end you will find Carter Lane, still medieval in character; shortly after the old choir school on the right-hand side of the road, you come to St Andrew's Hill. Walk down the hill and on the left you will find the church of St Andrew by the Wardrobe and opposite it the **Cockpit** (3). It dates from the sixteenth century and would certainly have been familiar to William Shakespeare, who bought a house nearby in order to be close to the Blackfriars Theatre, which was the winter home of the players who performed during the summer at the Globe Theatre on Southwark's Bankside. They used the buildings of the former Blackfriars monastery, abandoned after the Dissolution of the Monasteries Act of 1539. It is not difficult to imagine the crowing and screeching of the cocks in the fights to the death that took place here. Cock fighting was banned in Britain in 1849, and shortly afterwards this house was renamed the Three Castles after the three buildings of nearby Baynards Castle. However, a few years ago, it reverted to its original title and today the decor of the house features pictures of the old fighting cocks, and the bar has been arranged so as to recreate the pit and the gallery of the old cockpit of former times.

It is only a very short walk down the hill to the **Baynards Castle** (4) on the corner of Queen Victoria Street. Here the theme is medieval and revives the memory of the Norman fortress erected here during the time of William the Conqueror. According to Stow the first castle was built by a nobleman named Baynard who came to England with William. It was destroyed by King John in 1212 but rebuilt by Robert Fitzwalter later in the same century. When the Dominican (Black) Friars were granted land in the City in 1278 the castle was moved to a site opposite where the public house stands and there it remained until the Great Fire of 1666, when it was severely damaged. Parts of the castle were turned into houses, but in the last century all traces were removed. There is a fine model of the castle in the Museum of London on London Wall. A visit to the museum is worthwhile as it houses other mementoes of past inns and taverns of London.

Turning up Queen Victoria Street, part of a nineteenth-century road improvement scheme, you pass the British and Foreign Bible Society's headquarters, Faraday House, which when built in 1932 was called a disgrace on the grounds that its nine storeys would hide St Paul's Cathedral from view. The walker now comes to Godliman Street, at the side of the College of Arms, founded in the fifteenth century to grant coats of arms to appropriate people in England. Behind the College is Knightrider Street, once described as the longest in the City, when it led from the Tower of London to the King's Wardrobe by Baynards Castle. At the far end is the **Horn** (5), a building some two hundred years of age. Charles Dickens in *Pickwick Papers* has Mr Pickwick send his friends to the tavern to fetch a bottle of wine for his supper; today a marble bust of Dickens dominates the bar. Hidden behind the office blocks, the tavern is slightly off the beaten track for the tourist, but it is a must for addicts of Dickens. In company with some other public houses in the City it does not keep normal opening hours, closing at 9.30 p.m., and having only a five-day licence.

From outside the Horn, St Paul's can be seen once more and after returning to its south side, past the City of London Information Centre, Cannon Street is reached. Walk down the street and Mansion House underground station is on the right-hand side. Opposite it is Bow Lane. Go up the lane and shortly Watling Street crosses over. On the corner is **Ye Olde Watling** (6), whose sign proclaims 'Rebuilt 1666'. Photographs taken early in the twentieth century show the house as a restaurant, and this is in keeping with its original licence, which clearly says that a meal must be ordered before the drinks. Today the tavern is a pleasant oasis surrounded by the tall office blocks and shops of the busy City.

For one of the most difficult-to-find taverns of the City the walker must continue up Bow Lane: on the left-hand side is the entrance to Groveland Court and **Williamson's** (7). It stands in a cul-de-sac alley, as it has done for two hundred years, secluded from the hustle and bustle of life in the City. In the eighteenth century a certain Mr Williamson turned the house on the site into an inn or tavern. Sir John Falstaff had owned a previous house on the site. The tavern had a large lounge that was used as a banqueting hall, and many people think that this was the original Mansion House, official residence of the Lord Mayor of London during his term of office. However, there is insufficient evidence to satisfy modern historians of this, but it is recorded that in the late seventeenth century the Lord Mayor did entertain the king and queen, William III and Mary, here on one occasion. They brought the Lord Mayor a gift, a fine pair of wrought iron gates. After these had been presented to the Lord Mayor they were taken outside, but the queen promptly ordered their return to the hall.

Today they can still be seen, outside, at the end of the alley. One of the pub's rooms is called the Mansion House Lounge, and there is also a stone that declares itself to be in the centre of the City, though how this is measured is not stated. There is also a fireplace made from some Roman tiles that were found on the site during rebuilding after bomb damage in the Second World War.

The magnificent church of St Mary le Bow can be seen at the end of Bow Lane after visiting Williamson's. This end of the lane leads directly into Cheapside, which in medieval days was three times its present width and was the main shopping centre of the City. At the end of the lane turn right into Cheapside and after passing King Street, which leads to the Guildhall, and Ironmonger Lane, with the Mercers' Company Hall, Old Jewry is on the left-hand side of the road just beyond where Cheapside becomes Poultry. Here is the public house of the **Three Crowns** (8); its inn-sign shows the three crowns of England, Scotland and Ireland, together with the floral symbols of each kingdom, the rose of England, the thistle of Scotland and the shamrock of Ireland.

Return to Poultry and turn left to reach the Bank intersection. One of the dominant buildings is the Mansion House, built to the designs of George Dance the Elder at a cost of over £70,000 in 1752; Sir Crisp Gascoigne was the first Lord Mayor to use it, in 1753. Beside it is the street called Walbrook after the river that flows underground beneath it today. On the right-hand side is **Deacon's** (9), which has acquired a reputation over the years of catering for the younger generation, and where on occasions girls outnumber boys. It is built into Bucklebury House; during excavations for the foundations of the building the Mithraic temple of Roman London was found. The temple has now been rebuilt on the other side of the block in front of Temple Court, the offices of the Legal and General Insurance Company.

Cannon Street crosses Walbrook a few yards from Deacon's. Follow it towards London Bridge, to the **Square Rigger** (10), where the brewers have reproduced an eighteenth-century frigate in which to take refreshment. Rebuilt in 1963, it is complete down to the last seagull on the rigging above your head. Towards the end of a good evening in the place the sea takes on a slight swell, and the view out of the Captain's Cabin has a distinct lilt about it. The designer is to be congratulated on producing such an authentic-looking vessel.

The tall column visible from the front of the Square Rigger is the Monument, designed by Sir Christopher Wren to commemorate the Great Fire of London. It stands 202 feet (62 metres) high, the distance from its base to the spot in Pudding Lane where the fire started in the king's baker's shop. The column stands on the site of one of the first churches to be destroyed in the fire, St Margaret's, New Fish Street, in whose parish is also to be found the **Canterbury Arms** (11). It takes its name from the Canterbury pilgrims who started their pilgrimage to the shrine of St Thomas Becket from the chapel, on old London Bridge, which was also dedicated to the saint, who was born in London's Cheapside. There has been a tavern on this site since at least the fourteenth century, although the present building dates from the twentieth century. Among the unusual items to be found here are the Beadle's tricorn hat and his truncheon.

Finally Billingsgate Fish Market is reached, its presence becoming increasingly obvious as you approach because of the smell of the fish. Although the market has only been here since its royal charter was granted in 1699, it stands near the site of the original Billingsgate dock. Like the workers at other London markets, Billingsgate's workers have local inns and taverns where they can refresh themselves when other drinkers are barred by the licensing laws. At the river end of Lovat Lane, named after the last man to be publicly beheaded on Tower Hill, Lord Lovat, stands the **Cock Tavern** (12). Here the fish porters of Billingsgate may drink 'out of hours'.

13. Hard by the city wall

The city wall of Roman London, built in the second century AD, enclosed some 330 acres (134 hectares) and was over 3 miles (4.8 kilometres) long, thus making London the fifth largest city of the Roman empire. From the Tower of London it stretches in a rough semicircle to Cripplegate fort and down towards Blackfriars, before skirting the riverbank back to the Tower. Four or five different gangs of workmen built the wall, as can be seen by the use of different bonding methods in the various parts of the wall that are left today.

Fenchurch Street station was the first railway terminus to be built inside the city wall, in the nineteenth century, and it looks as if Sir Christopher Wren designed it as an orangery for a palace or country house. Where the railway lines cross over Cooper's Row, so named from the barrel makers who set up business here long ago, is Crosswall Street and the **Crutched Friars** tavern (1). Until the sixteenth century a monastery stood nearby. Its friars wore a large leather cross and thus were called the crossed or crutched friars. The inn's sign shows two friars wearing their robes, complete with the cross.

The **Three Lords** (2) in the Minories commemorates the last three members of the landed gentry to have been publicly beheaded on Tower Hill. In 1745 there was an uprising in Scotland in support of Bonnie Prince Charlie, who in the eyes of these three lords was the rightful heir to the thrones of Scotland and England.

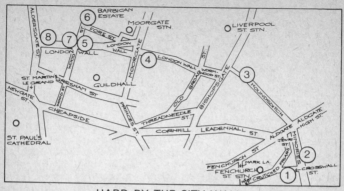

HARD BY THE CITY WALL

1. The Crutched Friars
2. The Three Lords
3. The Clanger
4. The Stirling Castle
5. The Podium
6. The Crowders Well
7. The Barbican Tavern and Restaurant
8. The Museum of London

Lord Balmerino was brought to London after the Battle of Culloden, charged with treason and condemned to be beheaded. The Earl of Kilmarnock suffered the same fate; his execution has been described as being a most just mixture of dignity and submission. Finally, Simon Fraser, Lord Lovat, was found guilty and became the last man to be publicly beheaded in England. The sign shows the three, together with the axe and execution block.

Keeping to the outside of the city wall, cross Aldgate High Street and walk along Houndsditch to discover a relatively new public house, the **Clanger** (3), at number 106. The decor, both inside and out, has as its theme the Great Fire of London; there are specially smoked beams in the saloon, and the London Fire Brigade is represented in the Brigade Restaurant upstairs, which has fire-engine red as the theme colour.

Entering the walled City of London by way of Bishopsgate, look for the two mitres, the special headgear worn by bishops, on either side of the roadway where once stood the gate erected by a former Bishop of London, St Erkenwald, in the seventh century. Soon Wormwood Street will be seen on the right-hand side; walk down the street, which shortly becomes London Wall, pass the Guild Church of All Hallows, London Wall, which was rebuilt in the eighteenth century, and the company hall of the Worshipful Company of Carpenters, with its charming arcade beneath, and find the **Stirling Castle** (4). Patronised by members of the Stock Exchange, it is said that it is easy to distinguish the day's winners on the Exchange by their laughter and congeniality.

Heavily bombed in the Second World War, the area around London Wall towards Cripplegate and Barbican has been subsequently redeveloped. Shortly after crossing Moorgate you will find Moor House, to the side of which is a flight of stairs that leads to an upper walk with shops, offices and a public house or two. As it is sited on the raised walk, it is hardly surprising that one of the public houses is called the **Podium** (5), derived from the Latin word meaning a balcony above the arena of an amphitheatre. It certainly has an arena before it, with the City stretching as far as the eye can see, and with the new housing estate of the Barbican behind it.

Using the stairs to one side of the house, descend to St Alphage Gardens and an extremely interesting stretch of the City Wall, showing all periods of its growth from Roman to Tudor times. Pass a blue plaque noting the site of the Cripplegate through the wall and Roman House, with its interesting mural showing the city in Roman days, and the Barbican Estate will be found. Just inside the area is the **Crowders Well** (6). The original well had a reputation for its medicinal qualities, and people from all over London came to take the waters. Today it has become a pub but the well is still there, although its water is not served to the customers.

Return to Wood Street and to London Wall. Close by the new Museum of London is the **Barbican Tavern and Restaurant** (7), from which a fine view of the herb garden of the Worshipful Company of Barber Surgeons can be enjoyed.

The **Museum of London** (8) has a number of items relating to the lost inns and taverns of the City of London, and among the exhibits is the inn sign of the Bull and Mouth, which once stood in nearby St Martin Le Grand, until the General Post Office pulled it down in the latter half of the nineteenth century. While the only refreshments available from the museum are tea, coffee and soft drinks, it is not an inappropriate place to end a walk in search of taverns and inns close to the city wall of London.

14. Legal London's tipple

Inscribed on a stone in Crown Office Row in the Inner Temple, on a building on the site where Charles Lamb was born in 1775, are the words:'a man would give something to have been born in such a place.' This is how Lamb expressed his thoughts on having been born in such surroundings, and he was rightly proud. For here, together with the Middle Temple, Lincoln's Inn and Gray's Inn, the 'men of law and their students' come to converse and to learn the noble art of law. This is indeed the university of law, as it has been for the past five or six hundred years. Full of intriguing corners, avenues and houses of all shapes and sizes, the Inns of Court have much to offer the wanderer among their leafy glades. However, the Inns are private and members of the public must abide by the rules of the Inns, which are clearly posted at the main entrances.

The **Ship** (1) in Gate Street is said to date back to 1549 — the date of its foundation is clearly shown on the outside of the building — but the present building is certainly not so old. However, the cellars, with their secret tunnels, did form part of the original house. During times of religious persecution Catholic priests came here to say the then forbidden Mass. On the approach of the forces of the law they would hurry down into cellars beneath the building and escape into the fields. The Guild of Fellowship Porters held its initiation ceremonies here; a new member had to redeem his badge by drinking a large tankard of ale without spilling a drop. The badge was dropped into the tankard before he was given it. In the seventeenth century the area was notorious for its immorality, which shocked even Pepys.

It is a pleasant walk down the west side of Lincoln's Inn Fields, passing a number of architecturally interesting houses, particularly numbers 59 and 60, designed by Inigo Jones, who laid out the Fields as a square in the seventeenth century. In the far corner is Portsmouth Street, whose most famous building is the Old Curiosity Shop. Its sign declares that the shop is the one 'immortalised by Charles Dickens', although there seems little doubt that this is not the actual shop site, which was where Irving Street meets Charing Cross Road today. But the building is an excellent example of sixteenth-century architecture. At the end of the street is the **George IV** (2) in Portugal Street. George IV reigned for ten years from 1820 to 1830 and during that time the streets around this neighbourhood were redesigned. It was in Portugal Street, in 1826, that stocks were last used publicly in London.

In Carey Street is the **Seven Stars** public house (3), whose original name was the League (or Leg) of Seven Stars, after the seven provinces of the Netherlands. Dutch sailors are said to have settled in the area in the seventeenth century and frequented the house. Today the clientele consists mainly of lawyers from the neighbouring Royal Courts of Justice. The house is said to have been built in 1602, making it one of the few surviving buildings that date from before the Great Fire of 1666. Scrutiny of the cartoons and other pictures on the walls of the comparatively small bar is well worthwhile in between drinks. This is another of the many London taverns that can claim close associations with Dickens and his writings.

It has been contended that the legal profession is a thirsty one, and there are certainly very many drinking establishments around the Inns of Court. In Chancery Lane the **Three Tuns** (4) displays

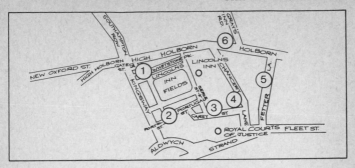

LEGAL LONDON'S TIPPLE

1. The Ship
2. The George IV
3. The Seven Stars
4. The Three Tuns
5. The Printer's Devil
6. Henekey's Wine House

three small tuns or barrels.

But if lawyers need to drink between their briefs, then so do the printers of the national newspapers. In the **Printer's Devil** (5) in Fetter Lane they can have a drink and at the same time learn the history of the trade. The interior decor of the house shows the history of printing in Britain by way of illustrations and small models. The title of the house is taken from the seventeenth-century term for the printer's errand boy. However, the inn-sign shows a demon playing havoc with the print, for which the errand boys were unfairly blamed. Today the food and drink attract the journalists and printers from the nearby newspapers, and long since gone are the idlers or 'fewters' who gave the lane its name.

Standing at the entrance to Gray's Inn is the original **Henekey's Wine House** (6) of 1695. It is a combination of a wine house and a public house, the former to sell wines, and the latter to cater for those who prefer long drinks to shorts. Apart from its unique triangular fireplace, dating from the early nineteenth century, a novel touch has been added in the form of the small cubicles provided for those who seek privacy while downing their pint or two. The house has a 'yard of beer' glass that holds 3¾ pints (2.13 litres), and many a bet has been laid on whether a person could drink the contents without spilling a drop.

Index